TALES FROM THE ANGLER'S RETREAT

---

*Fishing stories
from South Uist*

EDITED BY
MATTHEW CRAMPTON & DAVID PEUTHERER

David Peutherer, a Glaswegian, and Matthew Crampton, a Londoner, are regular visitors to The Angler's Retreat. Both owe much of their fishing ability, limited though it be, to the robust instruction of Billy Felton; and owe some of their waistlines, unlimited though they be, to the fine and abundant cooking of Marion Felton.

David and Matthew on Loch West Ollay, September 2008.

www.anglersretreat.net

First published in 2009 by Muddler Books. www.muddlerbooks.com
© 2009 Matthew Crampton and David Peutherer. v1.2
Design Matthew Crampton.

Extracts from *A School in South Uist* by F.G. Rea are reproduced by permission of Birlinn Ltd. www.birlinn.co.uk

ISBN: 978-0-9561361-0-7

This book is dedicated to Marion and Billy Felton
for their extraordinary services to anglers on the
Scottish Hebridean islands of South Uist and Benbecula

and

gratefully acknowledges Bruce Sandison's tireless and
selfless work over many years to help protect
Scotland's heritage of wild fish.

CONTENTS

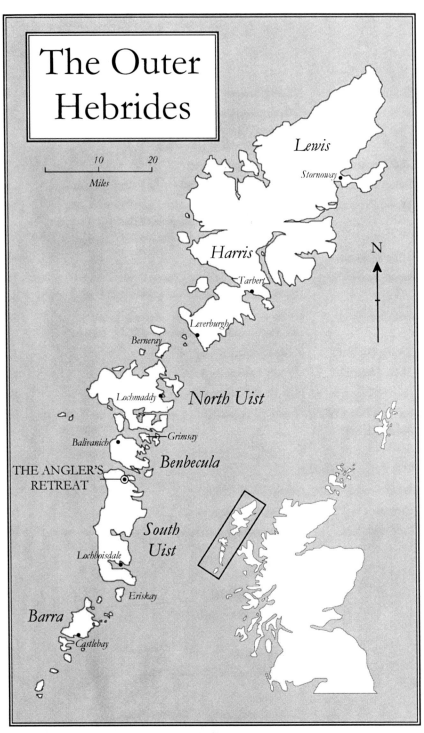

The Outer Hebrides

10   20
Miles

N

Lewis

Stornoway

Harris

Tarbert

Leverburgh

Berneray

Lochmaddy   North Uist

Balivanich   Grimsay

THE ANGLER'S
RETREAT   Benbecula

South
Uist

Lochboisdale

Eriskay

Barra

Castlebay

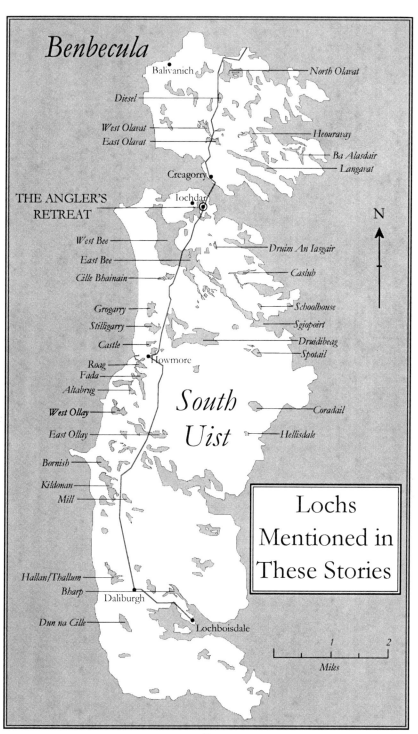

Benbecula

Balivanich

North Olavat

Diesel

West Olavat
East Olavat

Heouravay

Ba Alasdair
Langarat

Creagorry

THE ANGLER'S
RETREAT

Iochdar

N

West Bee

Drùim An Iasgair

East Bee

Cille Bhainain

Caslub

Grogarry

Schoolhouse

Stilligarry

Sgiopoirt

Castle

Druidibeag

Roag
Fada

Howmore

Spotail

Altabrug

West Ollay

South

Coradail

East Ollay

Uist

Hellisdale

Bornish

Kildonan

Mill

Hallan/Thallum

Bharp

Daliburgh

Dun na Cille

Lochboisdale

Lochs
Mentioned in
These Stories

1   2

Miles

SETTING THE SCENE

Imagine for a moment a remote Hebridean island so studded with game fishing waters it's hard to find dry land. Then picture a superb mix of quality-sized wild brownies lying in hundreds of shallow, lightly fished lochs where more than two people are a definite crowd. Nearby lies a sweeping coastline of silver sands and unpolluted aquamarine blue seas, fringed by green 'machair' lands covered in wild flowers of every hue. Sleek-backed otters and rare birds like the corncrake and the diver are your only companions. No, this is not an angler's 'fantasy island'. It is Uist, home of some of the best wild trout fishing in the whole of the UK.

Lesley Crawford

The Story of The Angler's Retreat

Matthew Crampton

Fishermen deserve good places to stay. Having shed vast sums on tackle, swallowed humiliating deals to protect their trip from family and office, and cajoled their fishing chums to do likewise, having appeased the logistical demon that puts prime fishing beyond easy reach and, finally, having staked all this effort on the lottery of good weather, surely fishermen deserve just one thing – their place of lodging – to be entirely dependable.

The Angler's Retreat is such a place. Its proprietors, Billy and Marion Felton, have created what many regard as the ideal guesthouse for fishermen. That's why the same names appear time and again in the Visitor's Book. That's why it's hard, even a year in advance, to reserve space during prime weeks in May and September. And that's why we've put together this book.

But what lies behind their success? What draws the fickle breed of fishermen to this pebble-dashed bungalow in the Western Isles? (Physically, The Angler's Retreat is a short, sturdy and dependable structure, just like Billy.) The answer is simple – you can depend on The Angler's Retreat. Billy and Marion have taken a lot of time to think about what anglers need, and don't need, then fashioned their hospitality accordingly. Anglers being largely creatures of habit, these needs revolve around straightforward things, like fishing, food and conviviality.

Fishing

When it comes to fishing, The Angler's Retreat is well placed at the top end of South Uist, handy for both this island and neighbouring Benbecula. A short drive brings you to some of Britain's finest trout lochs. And such is their variety, and proximity, that when fishing falters on one loch, you can easily move to another. Should the wind turn northeast after lunch, rendering your current location barren, you can shift to another spot which fishes better in such wind. Or when a gale has stirred your machair loch into porridge, you may find fish more amenable in a sheltered lochan nearby.

The trick, of course, is knowing where to go at what time. Billy's skill as a proprietor is not just to know the local fishing, but to steer his guests appropriately. After breakfast each day you'll find him poring over maps with a small knot of anglers – advising where's best for today's wind, how to fish each loch, where to drift and where to wade safely – patiently giving suggestions and alternatives until everyone is happy with their itinerary.

Crucially, he fashions his advice around his reading of each person or group. There are times when he will judge someone needs just to catch something, of any size, rather than labour long after something big. So he'll send them where smaller fish abound. Some groups refuse to wade, so he'll advise a loch with plenty of drifts. Other groups like variety – or might turn homicidal if spending all day in a boat together – so he'll suggest a location where they can wade, bankfish or drift as they wish. If anglers choose to pursue salmon or sea trout, Billy will also help them book lochs through the Estate. When time allows, Billy will come along as well, usually doing far

The Angler's Retreat.

more than his share on the oars and, as many of these tales testify, providing both valuable insight and fitting commentary upon the fishing skills on display.

Other than advice, there's fine fishing facility at The Angler's Retreat: plenty of space to store your rods and stuff; a drying room; appropriate flies to be bought at ridiculously low prices. Though only the foolish or ignorant would arrive in the Outer Hebrides without full kit and spares, should you become overdosed with misfortune – breaking both rods, perhaps, or holing both sets of waders – Billy will find some way to keep you fishing.

Yes, there's a danger his hospitality can be abused. This happens seldom, but it happens. Several regulars were present recently as two gentlemen of decidedly posh English demeanour displayed arrogance – and deceit – when returning broken an engine which Billy had lent them. But such lapses are thankfully rare. South Uist is the sort of place you don't need to lock your house or car. Most visitors embrace this trusting spirit.

Billy's garage is the epicentre of fishing activity in the guesthouse. It's where you store your rod, hang your waders and freeze your catch. Around you are the paraphernalia of sport: decoys for shooting geese, stumpy sea-fishing rods, empty ammunition belts, spare engines and inflatables, nets and seat cushions, creels and bass bags. You'll often find wild geese hanging on the back of the door, spoil from Billy's latest shooting expedition. The garage starts each season in neat order but by September, after months of ceaseless use, it becomes more 'Hebridean', as Billy would say, and stuff takes just a little longer to locate. But at all times it is a working space, with no frills, dedicated ruthlessly to helping sportsmen conduct their sport. As such, it provides anglers with what most fancy fishing hotels could never supply – the practical facilities you enjoy at home.

Food

On my first visit to Uist, I reached The Angler's Retreat in late morning – to be met by Marion with an unscheduled, unparalleled (and unbilled) bowl of homemade lovage soup. Wow, I thought, this place is a bit different.

Marion was put on earth to bring joy to men's stomachs. Twice a day, usually at 8.30am and 7.00pm, a group of predominantly men will sit expectantly in the dining room. Before them will appear dish after dish of unfeasible proportion. Conversation will quieten, plates will empty, then hymns of gratitude will rise up. Marion's brilliance in delivering meals of great satisfaction is central to The Angler's Retreat.

As a non-military person, I enjoy acquainting myself with the reassurance that comes with schedule. The plates are always hot. There are always three courses. Meals are always served on time. Marion will ask, then remember, what you want for breakfast. And it is comforting to enter this schedule – to make sure one is punctual – for it creates a backbone on which you can hang the day.

While there's a welcome routine to slot into, The Angler's Retreat also flexes to the god of fishing. Dinner time shifts according to season and to conditions. Marion will plate your food if the surprise or prolonged appearance of fish – or desperation to catch one – delays your return.

And the packed lunches! Forget those pathetic packages some hotels palm you off with. Marion's packed lunches have evolved through loch-side trial and error. First off, they're never housed in old supermarket bags which invite crushing; these come in sturdy plastic boxes, waterproof (of course) and see-through to ensure fair allocation (it's incredible how often people compare what they've been given, or become picky about bananas over apples). They contain enough food for several meals, because that's what stomachs like mine demand over the vast stretch between breakfast and dinner. There is no serviette. 'We tried paper napkins,' explains Billy. 'But they just cause litter – and who needs one when you're beside a loch?' And Marion will always fill a flask for you.

Yes, of course I eat too much when I'm there. And I suffer. After a huge dinner, when I rush from the table to fish through the Hebridean twilight, it's hard enough to squeeze back into my waders, let alone bend down to lace up my boots. But curiously I never seem to put on much weight during a trip. It must be the exercise and the air.

Conviviality

As you might assume, the guests at The Angler's Retreat are mostly male. And while there is much ribaldry, particularly the piss-taking humour that men favour, it is thankfully not a raucous place. Some people like to drink a bit, but most make do with just a glass or two. Women guests may startle at the men's capacity to discuss arcane fishing matters for hours on end but they would not, I believe, ever feel out of place. Again, it is Marion and Billy's triumph to create an inclusive environment, where people can relax in wholesome fashion.

And relax they do. The Angler's Retreat is a place of easy conversation and easy friendship. Marion and Billy always introduce guests to each other, with those staying one night given as much attention as longtimers. That said, people usually stay for a week. This gives plenty of time over meals to build a rhythm of sociability – of shared experience, storytelling and in-jokes – that leavens the sometime stress of angling.

Fishermen are a disparate breed. I, for example, have little desire to spend huge sums to helicopter onto some Siberian tundra. Colleagues often laugh at my lack of interest in tackle – my bottom of the range Greys rod has landed plenty of three pounders and I tend to use no more than six different flies during a trip. But I don't feel superior to those who do choose to hunt Siberian salmon, put the dearest technology in their hands and wield ten fly boxes. And we all seem to enjoy staying at The Angler's Retreat.

So, how is it that the Feltons have come to create this place?

History

Billy and Marion arrived in the Western Isles during 1981 when Billy – then a Sergeant Major in the Royal Artillery – was posted to the artillery range on Benbecula. In 1984 they went to live on a croft in Iochdar, a settlement near the north end of South Uist, easily accessible by causeway to the neighbouring island of Benbecula. On retiring from the army in 1995, they converted the house into a guesthouse and established The Angler's Retreat.

Prior to arriving on the islands Billy was primarily a coarse angler, though he'd started fly fishing on the Tees while posted in North Yorkshire. In Benbecula he attended a fly fishing course for soldiers run by John Kennedy and Brian Concannon. He learnt fast, supplementing the course with many days spent out on the lochs. When John Kennedy was posted outside the islands a few years later, Billy started running the course himself. Together with his son Fraser, he'd start his students off in January, teaching them the basics of entymology and tackle in the classroom. They'd use a gym for casting practice. Once the season started, he and Fraser (then aged 11) would take six students each out onto Diesel Loch and West Olavat – where fish tend to rise more freely – so they could cast for real. During the season there'd be plenty of practice so, by the autumn, the students would have a solid grounding in loch-style fishing.

At the same time, Billy – born in Plaistow, East London – became one of the few ever Cockney Crofters on the Western Isles. In 1987 ITV made a film about him for their 'Lone Furrow' documentary series. It's fun now to see a portlier, more hirsute army man – his nose still broken from his boxing days – looking after his sheep and cutting peat with the family. Incidentally the family includes three sons: Gavin, Danny and Fraser. Each went into the army, each became a Sergeant Major, and each has represented both their army and their country at sport.

Having made his commitment to the community, for buying a croft means much more than simply buying a house, Billy spent much time fulfilling that commitment. For many years Billy worked as secretary of the South Uist Angling Club. The Club fishes and sells permits on lochs owned by the local estate, now known as Storas Uibhst after it was bought out by the community. Though still working full time for the army, Billy was busy maintaining the Club's boats and organising its membership. For what happened next, I'll pass over to his fellow former soldier Brian Concannon:

'Billy was nearing the end of his military service and enjoyed the islands so much he was starting to look for things to do in his retirement. He and Marion lived in a three bedroom bungalow on South Uist with some crofting land. He thought about running a small bed and breakfast business while also doing some crofting. He discussed this with me and the problem was the lack of bedrooms for a sustainable B&B business. We went up into his loft and it was obvious that the structure was suitable for conversion. We then looked at extending the ground floor at the back of the bungalow to provide a guests' lounge, dining room, drying room and extended kitchen with a utility room. Billy and Marion decided to go ahead with this outline plan and consulted building experts to draw up detailed plans with a view to applying for planning permission. There were also grants available for the finance.

The building was completed and Billy wanted to focus on anglers as the main guests to enjoy the superb fishing of the Uists. They named it 'The Angler's Retreat'. It proved to be a great success.'

As you might expect of an army man, Billy was methodical in approaching this new occupation. 'I spoke to Harry Tannock and his son Paul, who used to run a guesthouse at Aviemore. I said, come and stay here. I'll teach you Uist-style fishing. You teach me how to run a guesthouse.' He made the most of courses offered by the army to those leaving the service, learning how to build and to decorate. 'But I never handle electricity or gas. Always bring in experts for that.' He learnt that one third of all new businesses fail in the first year, but those that succeed are often extensions of a hobby or interest. Hence Billy's fishing skills, and Marion's love of cooking, lay at the heart of the business.

Of course Marion brought much more than cooking skills to the venture. Having raised three sons, both on army bases and within the Western Isles, she was adept at organising a busy household. She got qualified on hospitality courses and for years delivered silver service in the Officer's Mess on Benbecula. Her roots, like Billy's, lie far from the islands. She's the product of Southminster, a small Essex town in an area long known for boatbuilding.

Together, Billy and Marion had a specific customer in mind. 'We wanted to create a place where working men could stay and fish,' he explains. 'It's expensive enough just to get to the islands, with the distance, the ferry and the cost of the petrol – and most fishing lodges cater for rich clients – so we opened a guesthouse which ordinary people could afford.'

It wasn't hard to find guests. Then, as now, there was a distinct shortage of fishing-oriented accommodation for visitors to the islands. While involved with the Angling Club, Billy had helped many people who wanted to visit there and fish. Plenty of those people stayed in touch – and now he could offer them a place to stay. Despite the original intention, these anglers come from all walks of life, a cosmopolitan clientele bound by a love of good fishing.

Along with fishermen, there are birdwatchers, cyclists and walkers, plus the inevitable human flotsam that washes up at remote b&bs. Most regulars can recall sharing the breakfast table with odd visitors to the islands – hippies in search of nirvana, mysterious salesmen and, most recently for me, an elderly Japanese woman who was 'walking' the islands with no rain-proofs, no walking boots and little English. She carried only a tiny backpack and a plastic bag containing a conical straw hat. She departed on a Sunday morning when, with the weather too harsh for her to walk and no buses in prospect, I dropped her off at the only place then open – the airport at Ballivanich. Until you've experienced the stark torpor of a rainswept Outer Hebridean Sabbath, even in the more relaxed south of the archipelago, you cannot appreciate the bravery, or foolhardiness, of visiting there without either transport or outdoor clothing.

It's similarly brave to open up your house to strangers. But the experi-ence, perhaps unusually for guesthouse owners, has been very positive. 'Before I started, people from the mainland told me that, in some places, proprietors have to screw their pictures to the wall,' says Billy, 'They said customers will steal whatever they can. But in 12 years I've not had one bounced cheque – and there have only been a handful of people I wouldn't ask back. Nothing's been stolen, except toilet rolls, and that's usually by cyclists.'

Now, after many years of incredibly hard work – eased by off-season winters spent being pampered in India – Billy and Marion approach retire-ment. At some point they will stop running The Angler's Retreat. This will give them the chance to spend more time living on the mainland of Scotland, where they feel the way of life is more relaxed than in England. They will probably settle in the area around Elgin which they love very much, from where it will be easier to visit grand-children in England. But their departure from The Angler's Retreat is a fearful prospect for the many anglers who have come to rely on it. For their creation is, above all, a dependable place. It is in tribute to that dependability – that bed-rock of hospitality within the rare richness of Hebridean fishing – that we dedicate this book.

An Introduction to Fishing on South Uist and Benbecula

David Peutherer

What is it about South Uist and Benbecula that draws so many anglers back there time after time? For some it is just the fishing, which is indeed excellent. But for others, including myself, it is the chance to combine this remarkable fishing with an inspiring and convivial setting.

Quite simply there are few other places, if any, where you can fish for Scotland's native brown trout by wading, bank and boat fishing, in so many lochs, most easily accessible, with such good prospects of success, and in such a beautiful place with proximity to so much wildlife and history. Crucially – and increasingly rarely nowadays – the fish on these islands are wild. No rainbows, no stocked fish of any kind. Just natural populations of brown trout which are beautiful, hard fighting and, in many of the lochs, exceptionally large. Add the possibility of a salmon, sea trout fishing which some experts rate amongst the finest in Europe, the fast-changing weather, the companionship of friends and the hospitality of Marion and Billy Felton – and the result is an experience not just special but, in many ways, unique.

This chapter seeks to place the fishing on these islands within the context of their wildlife, history and landscape. It is not a detailed guide to where to fish in South Uist and Benbecula. Anyone fishing there for the first time would do well to consult Captain John Kennedy's fine book *70 Lochs – A Guide to Trout Fishing in South Uist* which gives advice on specific lochs.

Wildlife and History

The wildlife is spectacular by United Kingdom standards. As your ferry approaches the east shores of the islands, you may see seals, porpoises, dolphins and occasionally even basking sharks and whales. The islands are one of the best places in Scotland to view otters and there is a population of around three hundred red deer. Moreover, the islands are renowned for their nationally and internationally important populations of both resident and migratory birds including ducks, divers, terns, swans, geese and waders. To watch a hundred or more swans take flight from East Loch Bee as you approach in a boat or along the bank is a magnificent sight.

Lapwings and skylarks, now seldom seen on most of the UK mainland, are quite common on the machair, as is the golden plover on the hills and moors. There are rare visiting species such as the red-necked phalarope and local specialities such as the Hebridean wren and song thrush. The elusive corncrake is often heard in spring and early summer, but seldom seen except by the luckiest angler or most dedicated bird watcher. Birds of prey – including short-eared owls, merlin, kestrels, peregrine, hen harriers and golden and sea eagles – are however frequently seen, often at unusually close range, as fisher and bird quietly pursue their respective prey.

The islands are rich in history, with archaeological sites dating from as long as 6000 years ago. You can fish amongst neolithic burial cairns, standing stones, iron age brochs, duns, souterrains and wheel-houses, some of them on man-made islands in the lochs. The remains of a bronze age village, complete with the only mummified bodies found in Europe, has been found beneath the sand dunes, as well as several Viking settlements. From more recent times there are the birth place of Flora MacDonald, Ormacleit Castle (home of the chief of the once powerful Clan Ranald), thatched houses and, as in so much of the highlands and islands of Scotland, abandoned crofting communities which provide enduring evidence of the effect of the 19th century clearances.

Such history gives rich texture to the fishing. It is a special thing to drift in a boat past islands which were made and lived on by people thousands of years ago – people who would have fished in the same lochs for the ancestors of the fish there now – while eagles soar overhead, a skein of geese flies over to neighbouring feeding grounds or an otter fishes nearby. But this texture would mean little if the fishing was not so good. And the main reason for the good fishing on the islands is the landscape, particularly the different fish habitats it provides.

Landscape

The landscape is remarkably varied for such a small place. A product of thousands of years of glaciation, and of action by wind, sea and people, it incorporates most of the iconic natural features of Scotland; the notable exceptions being forests and big rivers – this is near treeless terrain in which you fish almost solely in lochs.

Along the west coast there are miles of beautiful, unspoilt and usually deserted sandy beaches backed by high sand dunes. Behind and below these lies the machair. A gaelic word meaning a low lying plain, machair is one of the rarest habitats in Europe. Made of wind-blown shell sand covered with grass, much of it is still farmed in the traditional crofting way with cattle and sheep grazing between small fields of grain and vegetables. Early in the summer, the machair is carpeted by a multi-coloured profusion of wild flowers. Even the sternest, most focused anglers find themselves captivated by this sight.

Just beyond the machair, but before the moor, lie most of the island's crofting settlements. Scattered here on slightly higher ground, generations of crofters have improved the land by applying lime to reduce its acidity, and by replacing the heather with grass for their sheep and cattle.

To the east of the settlements, moorland covers much the largest part of the islands. Predominantly low lying but undulating and higher nearer the east coast, it is made of deep peat blanketed in heather. Largely unchanged for thousands of years, the moorland is a place of solitude and peacefulness, even quite close to the road, but especially for the angler who hikes off to distant lochs.

In the far east, in complete contrast to the west, there is a dramatic rocky coastline, broken by a multitude of bays, long winding inlets and narrow sea lochs. From this eastern side of South Uist rise the twin peaks of Hecla and Beinn Mohr, dominating the skyline for much of the islands. From their tops, on a clear day, you can follow the Outer Hebrides from Mingulay to Harris, then out to St. Kilda. Turning the other way, you can see the Inner Hebridean islands of Skye, Rhum and Mull and the mainland mountains of Morar and Ardnamurchan.

Fishing

Amidst all this beauty there are estimated to be between eight and nine hundred lochs. Each one can be fished, with a permit from either the local angling club or, in the case of the salmon and sea trout lochs and the very best of the brown trout lochs, from the community-owned Storas Uibhist Estate. There are so many lochs that, without access to John Kennedy's book or Billy's encyclopedic knowledge, first-time visiting anglers would not know how to make the best of their time on the islands.

So close together are the lochs in some areas, you need a map to navigate between them. There are lochs and lochans of all shapes and sizes. Many lie near the road, others require a short drive along rough tracks or a walk of up to an hour or so across the moor or into the foothills of Hecla and Beinn Mohr and, further south, of Stulabhal. Here you'll often be the only angler to fish them in twelve months or more.

A roadside loch. Simply park and cast.

So many lochs, so close together, gives the angler great flexibility. You can spend all day fishing one loch, or the daytime on one and the evening on another, or fish several in one day; similarly you can easily switch between wading, boat or bank fishing. Some people particularly enjoy a day walking across the moor casting a line into half a dozen or more lochs. There is no need to fish the same loch twice if you don't wish, or indeed to fish it twice in the same way. The angling club and the Estate between them have boats on around forty-five of the lochs, while many lochs are shallow and safe for wading.

On all of the lochs fishing is by fly only. Many anglers use traditional patterns of wet loch flies in sizes 12 to 10, with 8s for windier, big wave conditions, a bushy fly on the top dropper and a muddler or other hackled fly on the point. But there is more than one way of fishing here. Big fish can be caught on smaller flies; dry fly fishing and dapping can be successful, as can also be buzzers and nymphs in appropriate conditions. Only when there is a hatch of flies is it necessary to imitate a particular fly, and hatches happen here less often than elsewhere. Successful flies tend to imitate the small fish, crustaceans and sub-surface insect life which make up most of the fishes' food.

One technique not unique to the islands, but used very successfully here, is 'dibbling' the top dropper fly over the surface before lifting the flies off the water. This creates a wake and acts as an attractor, often resulting in a fish taking one of the other flies. Sometimes it is the dibbled fly which is taken. To watch a dibbled fly being followed then taken by a fish close to the boat is one of life's great angling pleasures.

Some anglers, used to fishing for rainbows in commercial fisheries, stand in one place for a long time casting over the same piece of water. That doesn't work on South Uist and Benbecula. Wild brown trout are territorial. Here anglers, like their prehistoric ancestors, must be hunters who seek prey wherever fish may lie, whether in open water, over submerged rocks, around islands, on the edges of weed beds or close to the shore. It's vital to keep moving, whether drifting, wading or bank fishing: 'cover as much water as you can' is one of the best pieces of fishing advice for these islands.

The lochs which lie on the machair are usually, and justifiably, regarded as the jewels in the South Uist crown. Here the shell-sand makes the shallow water naturally alkaline, enabling it to sustain a food supply much richer than in most Scottish hill lochs. Consequently the fish grow faster and larger, with fish of over three and even four pounds caught regularly and the average weight half or more of these figures.

Such is the quality of this fishing, few anglers can resist the challenge and temptation to spend at least a few days on the machair lochs. But these can be dour, moody places where it's common to blank – even a good day may bring contact with no more than a handful of fish. And when the wind blows hard, as so often happens in the Western Isles, it tends to stir up the sandy bottom of most machair lochs, rendering them soup-like and unfishable. Though should that happen, there are always plenty of alternatives.

The water is similarly alkaline in the lochs between the machair and moor, where the bottoms are also sandy and the surrounding land has been improved by liming. Some of these lochs perform almost as well as the true machair lochs. Even those with a lower average size of fish still produce plenty of two pounders or more.

Out on the peat moor the water is more acidic and the food supply sparser – hence the fish tend to be smaller. But conditions vary enormously, with some lochs featuring large populations of smaller fish and others having fewer fish but of larger average size. In any hill loch – including the unlikeliest looking – there may be monsters, as Robert Hannah shows later in the book, so it is worth casting into every loch you encounter. And on each visit it is worth trying at least one new one.

One reason why you can never be sure what you will catch is because many lochs are so rarely fished. Not surprisingly in these circumstances, some fish grow to a large size. Another reason is the intricate network of narrow burns and drainage ditches, crisscrossing the machair and moor, through which fish can move between lochs and share spawning grounds. Hence many of the fringe lochs, and some of the moorland ones, feature fish of the same stock, appearance and quality, though not necessarily size, as the machair lochs to which they are ultimately joined.

The same network of burns and ditches allows sea trout to move about, so these too can be caught in lochs not known for migratory fish. Elsewhere, particularly on the east side of the islands where the lochs are close to the sea and often brackish, sea trout move in to the lochs at high tide and can be caught both in the lochs and in the estuaries and sea pools.

You can often tell where a fish has been caught by its colouring. In some machair lochs the fish are predominantly light brown with the white bellies and red spots typical of all wild brown trout. Other sandy lochs produce golden, buttery trout – surely the most beautiful an angler may ever have the joy of catching – while those in the peat lochs are usually darker. All tend to take hard and fight hard. But sometimes the largest take with a gentleness which fools the inexperienced angler into thinking they've hooked something small – until the fish takes off at full speed, bending the rod, stripping line from the reel, diving and boring and, most exhilaratingly of all, leaping full length out of the water, sometimes several times in a row. You can only understand the excitement, and fear, this produces when you've actually experienced it.

Although sea trout can appear in many lochs, as can salmon, by far the best sea trout and salmon fishing lies in seven lochs – Fada, Roag, Bharp, Castle, Mill, Lower Kildonan and Schoolhouse. The main runs of fish begin in the middle of July and continue until the end of the season on 31st October. The number of salmon caught has increased in recent years but South Uist is not a prolific salmon fishery. Nor does it produce many very big salmon: most are grilse of under ten pounds. But it is not the size or number of salmon which attracts salmon anglers. They are drawn by the fact that South Uist is one of the few places where salmon can be caught from a boat on a loch using a single rather than double-handed rod.

Sea trout catches have, as in many other areas, decreased over the decades though numerically they are much better than the salmon ones. But it is the prospect of catching big sea trout which attracts anglers to South Uist and leads some experts to rate this amongst the finest sea trout fishing in Europe. Among the largest catches in recent years were a fish of ten pounds caught by Neil Patterson when Billy was ghillying for him in 2000, another of thirteen and a half pounds caught on Lower Kildonan and a fish of nine and three quarter pounds on Fada in 2007.

It is clearly very different to fish for salmon and sea trout in a loch rather than a river. But in at least one respect it is similar. As in rivers, loch fish do not lie everywhere, but are mostly found in specific areas where they wait until conditions are right for them to move up into the next loch or to the spawning grounds. Anglers unfamiliar with the lochs, or who don't have access to Billy's expert advice, should employ a ghillie who knows the lochs and who will make sure they fish the areas with the best chance of success.

Despite the best efforts of a ghillie, however, there are days on South Uist when even the most fanatical salmon and sea trout anglers might wonder what on earth they are doing there. Days when the sun shines from a clear blue sky, the midges are biting, the surface of the loch is like glass and there doesn't appear to be a fish within a mile of the boat. Or other days when a gale force wind is blowing, or it feels like it, when the loch looks like the Atlantic Ocean, hailstones are being driven horizontally into your face, your fingers are too cold to grip the line and you can feel water seeping through the back of the jacket which the salesman absolutely guaranteed was one hundred (and ten!) percent waterproof – and you realise that you have left your packed lunch and flask of hot soup back at the guest house.

Even when conditions look ideal, a week can easily be spent without making contact with a single salmon or sea trout. And, as Billy often points out, this is as true for experts as novices. Surprisingly often, the beginner gets the best or only salmon in a group.

So why do it? Maybe it's the anticipation that keeps you going – feeling that despite the weather, the midges and everything else, the loch is absolutely 'full of fish' because the ghillie has said it is and you believe him because you really want to. The ghillie skilfully positions the boat over one of the best lies in the loch. Your flies land just right on the water. You imagine the big silver beauty lying just below the surface, then the swirl and splash as it takes the fly. The rod bending, line tightening, reel screaming, arm straining, heart thumping excitement of the fight. And, if you are lucky, the incomparable satisfaction of netting a fresh run fish, then carefully returning it to produce future generations of fish as wild and natural as those your predecessors have caught on South Uist for thousands of years.

As if all this loch fishing wasn't enough, you can also fish for sea trout in the ford between South Uist and Benbecula, catch mackerel off the old pier at Loch Sgiopoirt, go sea fishing on Billy's boat, have lunch – and maybe a snooze – in the heather and look forward to one of Marion's dinners. It is easy to understand why so many anglers are grateful to Billy and Marion for helping them enjoy this wonderful place. And why so many return year after year.

THE HOSTS' TALES

Billy Felton is one of the UK's finest ghillies.
Stan Headley

*These are the real gentlemen, the keepers, stalkers
and ghillies . . . who have devoted all their energies to
providing their guests with sport and pleasure.*
Bruce Sandison

Billy's Tales

History of the Estate

The availability of good fishing and shooting on the islands was one of the reasons I was happy to accept a posting to the army range on the islands and come to live here in 1981 with Marion and our three sons, Gavin, Danny and Fraser. My association with the Estate and ghillying began when John Kennedy, then an officer and colleague in the army, left the island for a number of years and I was tasked by the army with taking senior officers and other visiting VIPs out fishing. Later, when John returned to the island and became Fishing Manager for the Lochboisdale Hotel, he asked me one day to ghillie for the Deputy Chairman of the Estate. Fortunately I was on holiday and so able to help. That, and my knowledge of the fishing, resulted in John asking me to ghillie for hotel guests when I retired from the army.

Ghillies were never employed by the Estate or the hotel. They were always, and still remain, self-employed. John Kennedy decided which ghillies were 'approved' and allocated them to guests staying at the hotel, but guests could also, if they wished, ask for a particular ghillie. I only ever worked part-time, partly because I had my army pension and other income, but also because Marion and I were running The Angler's Retreat and wanted to give priority to our own guests. I was also very selective about whom I would ghillie for.

Being a ghillie can be very hard work, particularly when there is a strong wind. It can be a lot harder when the client is 'difficult'. I wouldn't ghillie for anglers who I knew were unsporting, who wanted to kill every fish they caught, spent all day moaning uselessly about the weather, the water level or the fact that they hadn't caught a fish, or who didn't show any appreciation of the beautiful environment in which they were lucky enough to be fishing. On one occasion I stopped ghillying for a party which I learned had neglected to observe the Highland etiquette of tipping all their ghillies at the end of a holiday.

When I first became involved with the Estate, it was privately owned by an Anglo-Scottish business consortium which had bought it from a Greek gentleman in the 1950s. At one time it had been owned by Lady Cathcart. It comprised then, as now, about 80% of South Uist, 90% of Benbecula and the whole of Eriskay. Since at least the 1930s, it had been one of the best sea trout and brown trout fisheries in Europe, known particularly for producing large sea trout. It has never been a major salmon fishery.

Back then the hub of the fishing was the Lochboisdale Hotel. A traditional highland fishing hotel owned by the Estate but managed separately, this was usually full of fishermen throughout the season, because guests staying there had priority on the salmon and sea trout lochs and the machair brown trout lochs. John Kennedy drew up a weekly roster in which he allocated daily lochs to each guest. The roster was put up for guests on Sunday evenings and was a cause of great excitement, discussion and sometimes disgruntlement. The salmon and sea trout lochs are not equally good, so inevitably not everyone was happy with their allocation, but John always did his best to make sure it was fair.

At the end of each day when the guests got back to the hotel, they would display their catch on the slab, as was the usual practice in fishing hotels. It was not uncommon to see between six and ten good fish on show. Sadly the number and size of the sea trout has declined, as in many parts of Scotland, so fewer fish would appear on the slab, while the size of the brown trout has actually increased.
In the evening after dinner the guests and some of the ghillies would gather in the bar to swap stories and talk about their day. Many guests had been fishing on the island for years and so knew each other. It was a very sociable place, in the same way that The Angler's Retreat has been for our guests.

The hotel got into difficulties

Billy shows how it should be done.

financially when the number of guests declined. It was sold by the owners before the community bought the Estate and is now privately operated. Fishermen wanting to fish the salmon and sea trout lochs no longer have to stay there as the hotel has no control over the allocation of fishing. The Estate still produces a weekly roster, allocating lochs to fishermen irrespective of where they stay. Most of our guests come to fish for brown trout. Many of them want to spent at least a day or two on the machair lochs; some want to fish for salmon and sea trout.

The Estate has sometimes been criticised for not doing enough to improve the salmon and sea trout fishing. That is a bit unfair to the previous owners and John Kennedy, as John did produce a fishery improvement plan which they had said they intended to implement. But when the Scottish Government proposed legislation enabling communities to buy the land on which they lived, the owners decided it would be uneconomic to go ahead with the plan at a time when the estate might be bought: they might not get a price which reflected their additional investment. Hopefully now that Storas Uibhist (the new community organisation) has control of the fishing, it will carry out an improvement plan of its own.

The other aspect of the Estate relevant to The Angler's Retreat is the shooting. The goose and duck shooting are good, but the Estate is best known for the woodcock and snipe shooting. The Uists have arguably the finest snipe shooting bogs in Europe. Most shooters come in groups and stay at Grogarry Lodge, which is owned by Storas Uibhist, but some of our fishing guests also like to do some shooting during their stay, mostly for geese. Whenever I can, I arrange for them to shoot on the Ministry of Defence land at the range and, if possible, accompany them.

Because we have enjoyed living on the islands so much and because the fishing and shooting are such an important part of my life, Marion and I will always return to South Uist even when we move to the mainland. It has been a pleasure and a privilege to have been able to help so many people enjoy them as much as we do ourselves.

I am grateful to John Kennedy, ghillies Neallie Johnston, Donald Campbell, Colin McKenzie, Donald Gallagher and Iain Kennedy and the estate gamekeepers Alastair, Nigel and John for their help, friendship and, in the case of my fellow ghillies, their gentlemanly rivalry over so many years. Lang may your lums reek gentlemen.

The Brigadier's Scallops

When John Kennedy was posted outside the island in the 1980s, I started running the fishing course for the local angling club with my youngest son Fraser. Participants included serving soldiers and their families. We would take them to a loch, get them started fishing then take it in turns to walk round to see how they were getting on. One of the participants was Brigadier 'Bugs' Hughes who, due to a rugby accident, walked with a noticeable 'waddle'.

One day when I was teaching a group on Diesel Loch, a friend of mine drew up on the road beside the loch and gave me a gift of a dozen scallops which he had just caught. A few minutes later I saw the Brigadier walking round the loch towards me. He was some distance away but his waddle was instantly recognisable. Knowing that he had a good sense of humour, I decided to take advantage of the situation and put ten of the scallops in the back of my car and carefully placed the other two in the loch. When the Brigadier arrived beside me, he asked how the fishing had been. I said the trout fishing had not been too good but that I had had more success catching scallops. I showed him the ten in my car. The Brigadier then proceeded to look for some in the loch and quickly found one of the two I had planted. At that point I said I was going home. The Brigadier said he would stay to look for more scallops.

The next day I got a telephone call from the Brigadier's personal assistant warning me that I had better keep out of his way; he had been going round all morning muttering something about Billy Felton and scallops. Someone had obviously told him that scallops don't live in fresh-water lochs!

'Sea Trout'

A similar incident happened one time I was out night fishing with two soldiers who had attended one of the fishing courses, Regimental Sergeant John Ransom and 'Muscles the PT Buster' Pete Davis. We had gone down to the east end of East Bee hoping to get some sea trout which come in to the loch through the sluice at high tide. Pollack also come in the same way.

Soon after we started fishing I saw some pollack moving near the surface and, knowing that John and Pete wouldn't know what they were, told them to start casting over them. John quickly caught one and asked me if it was a sea trout. I said, helpfully, that it was. They went on to catch eight or nine each and returned home feeling very happy. The next day John telephoned me at work. During the ensuing conversation, numerous references were made to the dubious nature of my parenthood. I later discovered that they had taken their 'sea trout' to the army chefs and asked them to cook them. No doubt the chefs put them right about what they were, and had a good laugh at their expense.

Black Sam

When we were in the army, we liked to go fishing on Sundays. One time Brian Concannon, Lee Smith and I went to Caslub. In those days Brian had an old Seagull engine which was noisy, smelly and, crucially for this story, had no neutral gear so, unless you were very careful, it made the boat lurch forwards when the engine started. He also had a black labrador called, appropriately, Black Sam. Every time the Seagull started, its noise and smell would drive Black Sam into a frenzy of barking and snapping.

All this was generally bearable. Unfortunately Caslub features some dangerous sub-surface rocks near the boat station. Lee's job was to lean over the prow of the boat to look out for them while Brian was starting the engine. On this particular day, as soon as the engine started Black Sam became more frenzied than usual, snapping away at Brian's backside. This distraction made Brian less cautious with the throttle. It also made Lee less cautious with his look-out. I watched helpless as the boat suddenly shot forward, hit the rocks and sent Lee headfirst over the prow and into the loch. The moral of this story is: only allow well-behaved dogs into a boat.

(Nearly) Sinking with Lord Cranborne

One pair of VIPs I took fishing were Lord Cranborne MP and a serving army Colonel whose secondary job was army conservation officer. I knew they only had a short time to fish, so I took them to West Olavat. They arrived at the loch in a grand convoy consisting of the Brigadier's car, carrying the Lord and the Colonel, the Commanding Officer's car and the Regimental Sergeant Major's Landrover full of regimental policemen. When I asked the purpose of all these people, I was told it was to ensure the safety of the VIPs. I explained that such security was unnecessary in the Outer Hebrides; in any case they would be perfectly safe in the boat with me.

Back then West Olavat had a small boat with a bung in the bottom to stop water getting in. After we had been on the loch for an hour, I noticed a large puddle collecting beneath me. The Colonel had accidentally knocked the bung out with his feet, water was coming in fast – and we were in danger of sinking. So much for my reassurances about safety for VIPs. I quickly rowed ashore, feeling somewhat self-conscious. The next day I received a letter from Lord Cranborne on House of Lords notepaper, saying he had just sat through a very boring debate and his heart was still in the Hebrides. I didn't get a letter from the Colonel. Maybe he was embarrassed about not taking adequate precautions to conserve the life of his Lordship!

A Salmon, a Goose and a Bollocking

Another VIP who came to the range was Sir John Stannier, Commander in Chief of the military and the most senior officer in the UK. In honour of his visit it was decided to organise a day of shooting and fishing. John Kennedy arranged the fishing and got a salmon ready for him in case Sir John failed to catch one. I arranged the shooting and, on the day before, did a recce to establish where he would have a good chance of getting a shot, and shot one myself for him in case he failed to shoot one.

At the pre-shoot briefing at 4.30 am in the Commandant's house, I briefed the shooting party, consisting of Sir John and his two Lt. Colonel aides. I explained that I had prepared three hides – one for each of them with Sir John in the middle – and that I had laid out a spread of around twenty decoys to lure the geese in towards the hides. The plan was that just after dawn a small flight of about twenty geese would lift off and fly into the field area in front of the hides. I made it clear that, if this happened, Sir John should take a shot at them; but if they flew out of his range they should be left undisturbed, as the main body of geese would lift off later and flight into the same area, whereupon all three of them would get a shot.

Six geese duly headed in our direction and I could see from my position behind the hides that, if they kept on the same flight path, they would come well within range of Sir John. They did, but no shot was fired. Thinking that he had either fallen asleep in the hide or that his gun had malfunctioned, I crawled Indian-style to his hide, found him wide awake and alert and asked why he hadn't shot. He said he was waiting for the main flight to come in. I said something along the lines of 'For ****s sake that's not what you were supposed to do.' True to form, around a hundred geese lifted off later, flew towards the hides but then scattered in all directions when disturbed by two local shooters. Neither Sir John nor his aides got to fire a shot.

Around midnight that night, after Sir John and his aides had dined in the sergeant's mess, he got up to make a speech. He thanked the mess for their hospitality and said what a great day it had been. He had got a salmon which he hadn't caught, a goose which he hadn't shot and, for the first time since he was a young sub-lieutenant, he had been given a verbal bollocking by a sergeant major.

Sleeping Beauty

I was out fishing West Olavat with my commanding officer and we weren't doing very well. In fact, we were doing so badly he decided to have a sleep by the lochside. I walked over to the small loch just west of there, which often produces fish when the main loch is quiet. This day was no exception and I picked up a couple of fish around a pound and a quarter each. When I got back, the CO was still sleeping so I put the fish either side of his head and took a photo. 'Man Sleeps With Trout.' Then I hid the fish and said nothing of it. Months later at his leaving presentation, I produced the photo in a nice frame. He was very surprised. He spent the rest of the evening trying to work out exactly where I had taken advantage of him in this way.

Poachers

I was out one day with John Kennedy down the Carnan Road when we found a fishing net that had been hidden away in the heather. There was no doubt it was used for poaching. It was neatly folded and brand new, worth a bit of money, but capable of catching fish worth a lot more. We got some petrol and burnt it. A few days later I got a call from my commanding officer. Have you seen Loch Bee today, he asked. I said I'd not come past it that morning. Then you'd better go take a look at the boat station, he said. So I rang John Kennedy and we went down and found two of the boats had been turned upside down with their oars missing. An eye for an eye.

Sorting Flies

Sometimes you get so caught up in your fishing, you forget where you are – and how visible you are. There was an officer posted up here, a nice fellow with a very posh name, William Naismith of Posso, the Younger. One day he was fishing a loch just beside the road at Market Stance when he caught a fly in his backside. He couldn't reach it without taking his trousers off, so that's what he did. As he stood there, in his wellies and underwear – trying to sort out his flies – a bus went by, full of the women who worked for him on the base. They all gave him a sweet wave.

Bin Men

You see things on the Hebrides you don't see elsewhere. Bob Hutchison was fishing Lower Kildonan when a rubbish lorry pulled up nearby. One of the bin men jumped out, rod in hand, and started fishing. The lorry continued up a long cul de sac to service several houses. Ten minutes later it returned, picked up the fisherman – who'd managed several casts but caught nothing – and continued on its round.

Rivalry on Roag

James Paterson was one of the first hotel guests I ghillied for. There was always a friendly rivalry between him and his son Jeremy and they would frequently ask me, good naturedly, which one of them I thought was the better angler. I always said it was Jeremy, not just to wind up his father, though that would have been reason enough, but because Jeremy is flexible and adaptable as to how he fishes, while James is not. James will, for example, only fish with a floating line (no sinking lines or sink tips), use traditional flies (no muddlers) and will only cast in Scottish short-lining fashion. Because of this he usually, but not always, caught fewer fish than his son.

One year on Roag James caught a nice 4lb-plus grilse. The other person in the boat with James caught nothing and was none too pleased about it. I told him to fish the deep hole where the Roag burn enters the loch, emphasising he should use weighted flies to get down to the bottom where I expected the fish to be lying. He did this for no more than ten minutes before giving up, saying there were no fish there.

Later I advised Jeremy, who was in the other boat, to do the same thing and left him to it. After stopping for lunch at the boat station we saw Jeremy speeding towards us. When I looked through my binoculars I saw that he was grinning from ear to ear. I said to James 'I think you're in trouble here. I bet Jeremy has gubbed you again.' (*Gubbed* being Edinburgh dialect for defeated). He had indeed, having caught a 6lb grilse and two sea trout of 4.5lb and 3lb, all three of them in the Hole. I have to say that James was unusually quiet for the rest of the day.

The lesson which I hope the other guest learned that day is that, when fishing for salmon and sea trout, it pays to persist.

Don't Mix Fishing with Pleasure

There was a very different outcome another time I ghillied on Grogarry for father and son Paterson. This time Jeremy had brought up his new girl-friend. And, as the day proved, it doesn't pay to combine fishing and romance on the same holiday.

For the first part of the morning, while the girlfriend was off walking the machair, Jeremy had done better than his dad. He had caught two fish of a pound each. Now, with conditions becoming tougher, he thought it would be safe to take the rest of the morning off to join his girlfriend on the machair. So off he went, confident of his lead. But just before lunch James landed a fish of three and a quarter pounds, which we hid under the boards of the boat. When the loving couple joined us for lunch – and asked how we had done – we pretended the fishing had been terrible. So Jeremy, still thinking his two pounders would keep him safely ahead, now chose to spend the afternoon as well with his girlfriend, which he did. He returned as we were bringing the boat ashore and jauntily asked how we'd done. Not very well, we said, to which he joyously told his dad, 'Ah, you're gubbed again.' Then I said, 'Hang on, what's this under the boards', and I pulled out the three and a quarter pounder. That was a sweet moment. Jeremy just stared at it realising that, when it comes to competitive fishing, you just can't trust older men – or accountants for that matter – and you shouldn't become distracted by romance.

Danny and the Model

On one of my son Danny's leaves from the army he brought a very pretty Welsh girl called Debbie home with him. We later discovered that she was a model and had been a beauty queen.

Perhaps rather unwisely, Danny decided to take her to East Bee on a camping and fishing trip from the Friday until the Sunday. This made Marion and me smile because we had never seen Debbie until about eleven o'clock in the morning after she had 'done her face'. The thought of her going sleeping in sleeping bags used regularly by our three sons and their friends filled us with more than a little mirth. But off they went with all the camping gear.

Billy and Bee, on Bee.

When they arrived back on the Sunday they both said they had had a good time. But when Marion asked Debbie what she would now like to do, she made a half-spoken, half-screamed noise like 'Aaaaaaaaaaaaaaaaaaaaagh!' and said she had spent the whole weekend living with insects and midges, was covered with bugs and was going straight upstairs to have a bath. Danny said he had seen some sea trout jumping when they were on the way back, and promptly went back to the loch to try to catch some of them.

Captain Bill

Some of our guests are real characters. Bill is one of them. Eighty three years old but still very fit and as bright as a button, he was the captain of one of the cargo ships, or puffers as they were known, which plied between ports on the west coast of Scotland and the islands of the Inner and Outer Hebrides. He has a very infectious laugh and lots of good stories which he likes to share with our other guests at the dinner table, and in the guests' sitting room. He comes with one of his sons to fish but also shoots. I always try to take him goose shooting at least once when he comes to stay.

When goose shooting you must conceal yourself somewhere the geese can't see you. On one occasion when I took Bill shooting on the machair I told him to hide himself among some tall reeds at the edge of one of the lochs. It was a very windy day, so windy in fact that while Bill was 'hiding' among the reeds, the wind blew the reeds flat on the ground. Rather than being hidden he was completely exposed and the only way he could try to prevent the geese seeing him was to lie down as flat as the reeds. Another shooter wouldn't have seen the funny side of it but Bill did. He always has a good laugh when he tells that story.

On another occasion Bill spent the day fishing Langavat on the east side of Benbecula with his son Andy. Langavat is a narrow loch with a lot of small bays and is about two and a half miles long. The club boat is kept at the east end of the loch. While getting it ready, they noticed that one of the oars was split. As they had an engine with them they weren't too concerned about it. Not that is until the engine broke down at the far end of the loch and they realised they would have to row all the way back! To make matters worse, the split oar soon broke completely, so they couldn't row either. All they could do was paddle back, canoe-style, with the one good oar. As anyone who knows how strong the wind can be on the islands will appreciate, it was lucky for them they didn't have to paddle into an easterly wind. But their troubles still weren't over. When they eventually got back to the boat station they discovered their car battery was flat. One way or another it wasn't the best of days, at least up until that point in the late afternoon.

But Bill isn't one to become despondent; when he got back to the house he still wanted to go shooting. Earlier in the day I had reconnoitred the machair west of Loch Cille Bhanain on South Uist, noting where the geese were feeding and working out their probable flight path for returning to their roosting area. I put Bill in what I thought would be the best place for him to get a shot and the geese duly obliged by flying towards him. Bill shot three geese with two shots, only the second time he'd ever managed to do that. He was so pleased that when we got back to the house he did a little jig, laughing all the time as he did so. It's great to help guests have a success like that.

The Olavat Challenge

When there's a gang of people fishing, it's good to book the boats on both West and East Olavat. You divide into two teams, each fishes one loch in the morning, then swaps over after lunch to fish the other. You lunch together by the boat stations, weighing the team catch so far, then make a final weigh in at the end of the day. West Olavat tends to produce more fish, while East Olavat tends to produce larger fish.

One day I was fishing the morning on East Olavat with a friend and we'd had a few fish. At lunchtime we joined up with David and Chris, who'd taken a few more fish on West Olavat. David conducted the first weigh-in and declared his team half a pound ahead. Given that neither loch was fishing well, we fished hard that afternoon to catch up but drew a complete blank. So we'd lost, or so we thought, especially when we heard they'd managed another three quarter pounder that afternoon. But when David made the final weigh-in, he announced our team had won by two ounces. We said nothing. They bought the wine for dinner (which was the prize) and, after the first bottle, I gently asked if the figures added up. This prompted some urgent reflection in their team, especially when I referred to Chris's master's degree in maths....

During another Olavat Challenge, two guys from Lancashire in the other team were a pound up at lunchtime. Neither team caught anything during the afternoon so, as they were clearing their boat, they asked, 'Do you give up?' But I noticed a slight glance between them as they said this and, given my experience as a Sergeant Major, I knew that glance meant something wasn't quite right. So I demanded to see their fish from the morning, even though we'd already seen them at lunchtime. They sheepishly explained that a wave had washed away their bass bag which had been hanging outside the boat from the gunnel spiggot – and the fish were gone. You can never fool an ex-Sergeant Major.

The True Story of Neil Patterson's Big Sea Trout

Versions have been written of the circumstances in which Neil Patterson caught a 10lb sea trout on Fada in September 2000. As the person who was his ghillie that day, I want to put the true story on record.

Neil Patterson is a well known angling writer, a chalk stream fisherman and has experience of fishing for big fish. That September he and a party of anglers were brought to South Uist by Stan Headley, another notable writer and angler. The party stayed at the Lochboisdale Hotel and I agreed to be their ghillie.

One day I was ghillying on Fada for Neil and Stan. We had had a hard day with little reward. So in the afternoon it was decided to stop fishing and return to the boat station. At this point Stan, who had had a heavy night the night before, put aside his rod and reclined in the front of the boat, 'resting his eyes'. I started to row back to the boat station. Neil being a consummate angler rightly decided that he could fish while I rowed. He did this by side casting, using the 'turning flea' method whereby the angler casts out from one side of the boat, the line falls behind the boat as it moves forward and the angler dibbles the fly on the surface before recasting. The advantage of this method is that the fly covers a large area of water.

Halfway up the loch in the east bay, while Stan was still 'resting his eyes', Neil said he had something on the end of his line. I told him to take it easy until we knew what we were dealing with. Shortly after that a very large fish exploded from the water, the first of what were to be many jumps and many heart stopping runs. Neil controlled the fish expertly, using the skills he had learned from his experience of fishing for bonefish and tarpon, as I used my experience and knowledge of the loch to keep the boat in deeper areas and well away from weeds, rocky and shallow areas. During this period I vaguely remember that Stan, having stopped 'resting his eyes', was providing a running commentary.

After approximately forty minutes Neil had succeeded in tiring the fish out and was able to bring it close to the side of the boat where Stan netted it. It was a sea trout of 10lbs but not, as has been reported, a fresh run fish.

Neil, to his credit, wanted to return the fish alive to the water. I took the decision to kill it. This is not something I would normally do but on this occasion I believed that killing it and putting it on the hotel slab would not only be more convincing that such a large fish had been caught but would also benefit the hotel and the Estate.

The fish took a size ten Black Crow, a pattern devised by my friend James Paterson of Kelso. I had selected it and given it to Neil to use at ten o'clock that morning before he and Stan started fishing. He had used it all day, which is surely a lesson that there is no need to change flies frequently, or to change one, like the Black Crow, which you know consistently catches fish. A good fly will always, eventually, tempt a fish.

A few years later I read a magazine article in which Neil, when asked which of all the fish he had caught was his most memorable, said it was the sea trout he caught that day on Fada. That gave me a great deal of pleasure.

A Shrine to Smoked Trout

Marion and I are often asked about the small shrine-like structure at the bottom of the garden. It is actually the remains of a fish smoker. I only kill fish to eat and one way we and our guests like to eat them is smoked. When I mastered the art of hot smoking some years ago, I built the hot smoker at the bottom of the garden to keep the smell of the burning wood away from the house. For hot smoking you put the wood shavings and the fish in the same compartment, behind a closed door. The compartment has through-ventilation which creates a draft from bottom to top – so keeping the wood smouldering and the smoke blowing over the fish. You need to top up the wood with two or three handfuls of shavings every two hours or so; and it's very important to get the quantity and timing of these top-ups right.

One day when I was going to be away ghillying all day I had started smoking some fish before I left, knowing that our friend and builder Ron Macinnes was going to be doing some work on the house and confident that he would happily help by topping up the wood shavings. I carefully explained how many shavings to add and when to do so. Ron decided to save time and effort by putting on six hours worth of shavings, all at the same time. When I got home I discovered that the wooden door and the fish had both been reduced to ashes. To this day the smoker remains, as Peter Cook might have said to Dudley Moore, notably deficient in the door department, to the tune of one door.

Billy's Favourite Lochs

I have caught so many fish of all sizes that to enjoy fishing now I don't need to catch anything, let alone anything big. I enjoy helping my guests to catch fish of course, but my favourite lochs are ones which have other qualities, particularly peace and isolation, and interesting plants, birds and other wildlife.

I first got to know **East Bee** well when I moved to South Uist from Benbecula. I'd head there in the late evening, and stay out until one or two in the morning. Just me and the dog. Then I started taking the boys camping there at the weekend. Late on Friday afternoon we'd load up both boats with kit then take them across the loch, through the Cut and set up camp by the islands just southeast of there. As the water's brackish, we would have to carry all our drinking water with us. We would dig a tin box into the ground to serve as a fridge for what we caught. We'd walk over to Shell Loch, fish until dark then come back and cook dinner. At first light we'd take a boat down to the Sluice End and fish there. It was the best way to get to know a loch as you're there through all conditions and you can see how the fish respond to the changing time, tide and weather. We'd return on Sunday evening.

Bee trout are a bit different from other fish on the island. They seldom eat flies as there are no real hatches on the loch but, because it is brackish, there is an abundance of sub-surface food such as shrimp, lugworm, mussels and sticklebacks. That's why you need a longer retrieve on Bee than other lochs; it helps you cover more water and it better simulates a small fish. I don't necessarily strip faster on Bee, but I certainly cast further. Wading can be good, but it lessens your options. If you're in a boat and the Top Loch isn't working, you just head to Middle, then Shell. Blank days are very seldom on Bee.

Bank fishing down at the south-west end of East Bee.

Much has changed on Bee over the years. Now there's often too much weed in Middle Loch as there aren't enough swans to keep it low. Once maybe 300 swans would be there. That said, there are still a lot of swans about, plus eagles, peregrines, teal, widgeon, red stags, otters. There's always something to see on Bee.

During the 1930s there were six boats on **Langavat** and it was known for the finest sea trout on Benbecula. Now there's only one boat, rarely used.

Few sea trout are caught on the loch these days, but there are plenty of free rising brownies. It's not unusual to catch 60 in a day. Nothing of great size, but they give good sport in a beautiful setting. As you go down this long, thin loch, you can see how it has been split by the Ice Age. It's a place for Great Northern Divers, both black and red throated, hen harriers, sea eagles and red deer.

North Olavat is another loch that's fished much less these days, mostly because there's no longer a boat on it. North Olavat's trout tend to be larger than West Olavat but smaller than East Olavat and there is an outside chance of getting a sea trout. The fishing can be hard unless you know the loch well but it has lots of skerries and nice bays, and is very isolated and peaceful. I often used to take my kids there – it was where Fraser first hooked and landed three trout simultaneously. It has a lot of good memories for me. I hope the Club will put a boat on it again soon.

I used to love fishing **Caslub**, but it needs a decent boat. There are some good fish in it, including slob trout and sea trout up to 1.5 lbs. Fraser caught his first 2lb trout on it when he was 12 and I saw my first sea eagle there. In spring the islands are covered with bluebells and they have rabbits on them. I have always wondered how they got there.

I often used to visit **Fada** on North Uist when it was owned by the Department of Agriculture and Fisheries. As the boat station was half a mile from the road, we would carry the seagull engine, Zulu fashion, on a pole between two of us. It's a huge loch, where it's easy to catch 40-50 fish. It also holds arctic char, but I have never caught one.

Ba Alasdair is another beautiful loch full of bays, inlets and narrows. It is about a twenty minute walk to get to, but well worth it as you can get a bag of twenty or so fish mostly up to 1.5lbs, but with a chance of a slob trout or sea trout up to 2lbs. You can also collect mussels from the shore. It is one which you need to fish from a boat.

East Olavat has fewer, but on average larger, fish than West Olavat. It offers great variety – long drifts, rocky shores and skerries, bays, narrows and island shores. The wild life is outstanding too. It is the best place on the islands to hear cuckoos in the Spring when there are also grey geese gosling on the islands and it is quite common to see hen harriers. Look out also for water lilies in the spring and blackberries on the islands in September.

Billy's Favourite Uist Flies

GREEN PETER
Hook Size 10 or 12, long-shanked **Body** Green seal's fur with a slip of dark green olive feather fibres over the back, wound down on to the body by ribbing **Rib** Gold tinsel **Wing** Dark speckled fibres from pheasant wing, to lie along the sides in pupal fashion **Legs** Mallard scapular feather fibres or a few turns of ginger hen hackle

The Green Peter is an emerger pattern. Years ago it was one of the most popular and successful flies on South Uist, especially on the salmon and sea trout lochs. I have always liked the look of it and had plenty of success with it, particularly early in the season. Fish it on the point.

TEAL, BLUE AND SILVER
Hook Sizes 10 or 12 **Tail** Golden pheasant tippets **Body** Flat silver tinsel **Rib** Fine silver wire **Wing** Teal flank feather **Hackle** Bright blue cock

I use this fly on the point in brackish water and anywhere else there is a chance of getting a salmon or sea trout. Otherwise for salmon and sea trout I use a Stoat's Tail or a Dunkeld.

GREEN FRENCH PARTRIDGE
see Brian Concannon

Marion's Tales

Weather

Most of our guests and all our regulars are anglers but during the season we also get birdwatchers, cyclists, walkers and general holidaymakers. It is the cyclists we feel sorry for. Most of them come to the islands with the intention of cycling from Barra to Lewis or the other way round. Some are well prepared but others don't seem to realise how strong the wind can be, or how heavily the rain can fall, sometimes even during the summer. If they are lucky the wind is behind them all the way. But if they have to cycle into the wind it can be very hard work, especially if there is horizontal rain blowing into their faces too.

We always try to take cyclists in if they ask for accommodation. On one occasion when all our rooms were full, a girl came to the door. It was a really horrible day; she looked as if she was soaked to the skin and completely exhausted. We felt so sorry for her that we couldn't possibly turn her away. We took her in and let her sleep on the couch.

Marion and Billy

At least she got as far as the house. Another time the son of one of our friends came to the islands with his girlfriend and another girl. They thought they would be able to cycle all the way from Barra to Lewis in two days, which really wasn't nearly enough time, particularly since neither of the girls had cycled for a number of years. They had said they would call in to see us on the way past but they didn't get as far as here, at least not on their bikes. By the time they got to Howmore one of the girls had such a sore knee from cycling into the wind that she couldn't go any further. They had to give up and get a bus from there to Lewis. We never did see them.

Another thing first-time visitors do not realise is how quickly the weather can change. One couple who were on a camping holiday went to the west coast of the island to see the machair and the beaches. They thought the view of the sea from the dunes was so beautiful that they pitched their tent on top of one of them. That might be a good idea in some places, but not on South Uist. It was a lovely calm evening when they put the tent up, but during the night while they were asleep, the wind became so strong it blew the tent down on top of them and broke one of the poles. We were able to put them up for a night and dry all their clothes and equipment. Billy even found an old tent pole in the garage which he gave them so that they could continue with their holiday. The fact that Billy managed to find something in the garage will surprise people who know what it looks like during the season. But this proves he is right not to throw things away, even if the garage does look ever so slightly untidy!

Stray Possessions

It is amazing what people leave in the garage. Over the years we have found all sorts of fishing equipment. I think it happens because our guests are keen to fish for as long as they can, so they leave packing to the very last minute – and then don't have time to make sure they have taken everything. We always let them know if they have left something behind, and post it on to them or keep it until their next visit if they prefer. Things get left in the rooms too of course. Once I found a whole drawerful of socks and underwear which I washed and returned. Another time Val, who used to work for us, found a piece of equipment for testing the owner's heart rate. It was in one of the upstairs rooms. Val couldn't resist trying it. I still remember being downstairs and hearing her shouting, 'Oh my God I think I'm dead.' She hadn't realised it had to be switched on!

Cutting It Fine

Val was also involved in an incident involving a personal friend of ours who was staying with us. He was a very senior officer in the Indian army, a colonel and very particular about his appearance. Although he was here on holiday, Billy told him he should go to the army base on Benbecula to pay his respects to the commanding officer. Being a former Sergeant Major, of course Billy told him to get his haircut before he went. We don't have hairdressers' shops here so Val offered to cut his hair. He sat down and, just as she was getting ready to start, asked Val if she cut hair often. She said she had never done it before, which was true. It gave him such a shock that he almost leapt out of the chair. His face was a picture.

The Other Woman

Another guest had a shock of a different kind when he got home after a visit. He came here for three weeks every year and I did his washing for him. One time I washed his fishing trousers, which were very dirty from sitting about in boats all day. When he got home he said his wife was surprised how clean they were, so much so that she made it clear she thought he'd been playing away from home, and this other woman had cleaned his trousers for him.

Unusual Demands

We have got used to strange requests over the years. Quite a lot of couples prefer single beds, but one couple, who had got married when she was eighty and he was seventy-five, didn't just want separate beds, they wanted beds in separate rooms. They said they didn't share a room because she snored so loudly he wouldn't get any sleep in the same room. Every evening after they had gone up to bed, I would hear them creeping through the upstairs sitting room to each other's door and saying 'Goodnight darling.' I used to go to the bottom of the stairs and shout 'I can hear you!' They weren't a bit embarrassed and always laughed about it in the morning.

We haven't been able to agree to everything guests have asked for. In particular I had to say no to one person who wanted to bring a dog. I explained the arrangements about kennelling guests' dogs. She said she wouldn't need a kennel as her dog always slept not on but IN the bed with her and asked if that would be all right! I had to tell her it most definitely would not be all right. I don't know if she found anywhere that would allow it. If she did, I hope none of our regulars ever has to stay there.

This reminds me of another story involving dogs. A lady from Stornoway booked our caravan for a week: for her, her three children and three dogs. One day after they had all been down to the beach she came over to the house crying because one of the dogs, an alsatian, had died. Billy was home at the time and offered to bury it but she said no as she thought the dog would be happier if it was buried in Stornoway. She put it in a black plastic bag and kept it in the Nissan hut until the day they went home. They left in her car: with her, three children, two live dogs and one dead one in a bag, on a hot day in June! I can understand why she did it but I wouldn't like to have been in the car that day.

When the Scottish Government announced a ban on smoking in public buildings, including guest houses, we decided to do this a year in advance. Bill and George, who were two of our regular guests and both smokers, said they might have to consider staying somewhere else. So, because we knew they enjoyed staying with us, and we didn't want them to have to go elsewhere, Billy and one of our friends made a bench outside the guests' entrance, so guests could smoke in comfort surrounded by honeysuckle and other plants. The next time they came up Bill said the bench was good, but they were getting wet sitting there in the rain. Billy said that was no problem, gave him a sou'wester and told him to wear it every time he went out for a smoke. Bill and George still come every year.

Refreshments

We let guests bring their own drinks to have with dinner or later in the evening. Billy and I sometimes provide a bottle of wine at dinner time too when we eat with our guests, which we often do. Few guests drink much, but I do remember a few alcohol-related incidents.

One group of four regulars spend every evening after dinner playing cribbage and always bring their supply of drink for the week with them:

twenty bottles of wine, six bottles of port, four bottles of Baileys, several cases of beer – and a whole stilton cheese. One morning one of them told me he couldn't go fishing because he had a 'hangover from hell'! With that much drink to get through, I'm surprised he ever went fishing at all.

Another group used to go to the Dark Island Hotel on Benbecula for a drink later in the evening. On one occasion they came home late when everyone else had gone to bed. The drink had made them peckish. Next morning I discovered that they had eaten all the chicken drumsticks which I had been planning to give the guests in their packed lunches. I always have plenty food in the house so I was able to put something else in the lunches, but they were very embarrassed about it.

There was also a group who used to drink a mixture of Buckfast and Red Bull, although they were not the kind of people you might normally associate with Buckfast. They were nice lads but did tend to get a bit merry. When they were leaving one of them gave me a bracelet and watch, which was very kind of him. The only problem was that, while I don't know what they were made of, I do know that wearing them made my arm turn blue!

Rubbery Meat

They say lots of people behave differently when they are on holiday. I think it is because they are more relaxed when they are away from the stress of their jobs. We certainly sometimes see the other side of people's characters. One American who came a number of times with a friend was the high flying chief executive of an American-owned company in Scotland. He was obviously very serious and hard working at work, but here he liked playing practical jokes, particularly on Billy. One morning he put some golf balls under Billy's car seat cover. As Billy was in a hurry to get to a loch that morning, he had to drive all the way there sitting on top of them. He was none too pleased about that but appreciated the joke and decided to get his own back. I had made individual cottage pies for dinner that evening. When Billy got home he put a golf ball in the bottom of one of the pies. Afterwards the practical joker said that although he enjoyed the pie he thought some of the meat was a bit rubbery.

Helpers

We have been very lucky with the people who have helped us in the house. Norma who used to help with the cooking was very good with the guests and they all liked her, but she didn't like anyone else in the kitchen when she was preparing meals. Sometimes she got a bit confused when Billy or I did come in, particularly when she was filling flasks for guests' packed lunches. Guests would find they had tea instead of coffee, or even a mixture of both in their flasks! She would get the breakfasts mixed up too. If guests are having a cooked breakfast we ask them to fill in a chitty to let us know what they want, bacon, fried or scrambled eggs, tomato and so on. Sometimes they wouldn't get all they had asked for, or, just as often, they would find more than wanted on their plate. We always managed to sort it out and no-one ever went hungry.

Obviously we don't usually go away during the season, but when we have had to for a few days for family reasons, our friend Dolly looks after the guests. When we are away during the winter her daughter Donna helps by taking telephone bookings. Another friend Rick, who used to deliver our coal, did it before Donna. He used to stay in the house and look after the dogs too. We have been very lucky to have such good friends living locally.

Conviviality

One of the best things we did when extending the house was provide the sitting room for guests. They all use it but particularly the anglers. For them it is a combination of military-style operations room, for planning their day's fishing in the mornings with Billy, and a social centre in the evenings. Many regulars come at the same time each year, so a lot of them know each other. Most evenings they sit in there talking about what kind of day they have had, other places they have fished during the year since they last met, swapping experiences and telling jokes and lots of stories. Of course they come here mainly for the fishing but, for a lot of them, the socialising is an important part of their holiday.

Over the years we have had quite a number of parties in the sitting room. Some of them have been birthday parties for guests. We always give them a cake and a bottle of champagne or wine but we like to have a party too and sometimes, if it is a Saturday evening, we invite some of our friends round. Some evenings turn into ceilidhs with friends and guests playing instruments, singing and even dancing. Everyone enjoys these evenings, including Billy and me, because we like having people in the house, making people feel welcome and doing as much as we can to help guests enjoy their holiday. When we know we have honeymooners coming, we put a bottle of champagne or wine in their room.

Running the guest house has been hard work but we have really enjoyed doing it. We are lucky in being open for only around six months a year, as we can do other things during the winter, particularly see our family, visit our friends in India and, more recently, spend time in Morayshire on the mainland. But the most enjoyable thing about The Angler's Retreat is that we have met so many lovely people, made so many good friends and had so many good times with them. We are very grateful to them for supporting us and glad they have enjoyed their stays so much that many keep coming back.

THE GUESTS' TALES

By choice, one fishes alone. But it is curious to think how many
of the happiest days of your life have been spent in the company
of more-or-less complete strangers, united only by an obsession.

Jeremy Paxman

Ken Arfield

Livingston

Boatmanship

When you stay at Billy's for a week, he will do his best to get out for a day with you on a boat. The man has a real liking for East Loch Bee, as does my fishing partner John B. Personally (up until recently) I saw the loch as a big, salty, weedy waste of time. That changed this year when we had several trips on it and the conditions were superb – a warm west wind with fish bubbling everywhere and keen to take the fly. I even managed to land one from the Hole – the first time I wasn't broken there. The fish was a beezer of 2lb 2oz, smallish by Bee standards, but it made my day.

Anyway, back to my story. A few years ago we were up for our usual June week and Billy arranged for us to fish East Bee, with him accompanying us. Apparently we were to take turns on the oars, one rowing and the other two fishing. I assumed my turn on the oars would be a nice hour's rest, smoking fags and sitting peacefully in the middle of the boat. Well, I got that wrong.

Billy's a man of strong feelings but few words. Every now and then he would shout 'Kenny, the boat's bolloxed'. That's all. I assumed he meant the boat was sitting wrong in the wind and I should fix it. But he provided no further instruction. So I'd try one thing, and he'd say 'It's still bolloxed.' I'd try something else. 'Still bolloxed.' By my third turn on the oars, by trial and error, I was getting the hang of them, but if Billy had been a bit more instructive, I'm sure this would have happened earlier.

The fly for East Loch Bee is The Black Crow. When Billy gave us this pattern I thought he was taking the mick. But I tied them, we tried them – and caught so many fish that by the end of the day they were in tatters. That night we hastily tied some more for the next day. Fish it on the bob, you won't be disappointed!

> ## THE BLACK CROW
> **Hook** Size 10 B175 long-shanked **Silk** Black
> **Tail** Claret pheasant tail or cock hackle fibres
> **Palmer hackles** Black and scarlet mixed

Stuck in the Mud

Myself and my steady fishing buddy John B are regulars to South Uist, but this year our friends John W and Jimmy C asked to tag along, and we thought, why not? The week they picked wasn't that great as a cold north wind blew for the entire trip, so our friends didn't get to see the islands in the best light. Billy did his usual best and put us onto lochs that would have a bit of shelter from the worst of the wind, but even he couldn't do anything about the temperature.

One day he managed to get us on loch Thallum (aka Hallan), which is one of John B's favourites. As usual, Billy warned us not to wade on the right of the loch due to the very soft bottom. John B heeded this advice as he does every time, but John W didn't.

I was in the boat with Jimmy C and, after an hour, we finally located fish and started to get some sport. But this was to prove short-lived. Jimmy's mobile rang with John W on the line, crying "I'm stuck in the mud up to ma baws, you'll need to come and pull me oot!' We asked if he could wait 15 minutes or so as our sport was good. His reply was not fit for print. So we went and dragged him out and calmed him down but, on our return, the sport had died off again. If there is a moral to the story, I suppose it would be turn off your mobile phone when you go fishing. Your mate might drown but, hey, your sport will be better. Or maybe not.

> ## THE GREEN IMP
> **Hook** Size 10-16 B175 **Silk** Black butt green globrite #12
> **Body** 1 strand peacock herl (short dressed)
> **Rib** Fine pearl tinsel 2-3 turns only **Hackle** 2 turns black hen
> *This is a killer fly for the middle dropper or the tail of*
> *a three fly cast for early June on Thallum.*

The Golden Eagle

It's pot luck whom you share the Anglers Retreat with. If you are lucky, then there are like-minded anglers who enjoy a story and a dram and are easy to get on with. But sometimes you are not so fortunate. One year there was a fishing/bird watching husband and wife staying there. His name was Charles, but we could never remember her name, so we nick-named her Dave. To us they became Chas & Dave, so called because they liked to rabbit!

They were obsessed with trying to see a golden eagle, so each day Billy would put them on a loch for this reason more than for the fish. We, of course, were only interested in fish. But as fate would have it, we saw an eagle first. Billy had sent us out to Loch Heouravay where, at around midday, a golden eagle flew majestically over our heads.

Later on at supper time when Chas and Dave were recounting what they had spotted that day, and bemoaning once again the lack of eagles, we casually mentioned what we'd seen. That didn't go down too well with them and they gave Billy the third degree as to why he hadn't sent them to Heouravay. You can't please everyone can you?

BILLY'S BOB FLY
Hook 10-14 B175 silk black **Body** Black seal's fur
Rib Oval silver tinsel **Palmer hackle** black cock
First throat hackle Pink hen
Second (final) throat hackle Natural Gallena*
as we say in fly tying circles –
if you can't get Gallena, just get guinea fowl!

Roy Bartle

Billy's Fancy

When the fishing is a little dour, Billy can keep fishermen entertained for hours from his vast fund of stories. It is also necessary to know that Billy has very positive views on some things in life!

This much told story revolved around the time Billy arrived home one evening after a hard day on the loch. He found that during the day Marion had booked in two cyclists for a night's dinner bed and breakfast. When they appeared for dinner, they were dressed in pale blue and pink lycra outfits 'and that was not even their * * * * * cycling gear' as Billy expressed it. Billy's reaction to this sartorial picture was predictable, and I leave you to imagine his description of his feelings.

I have to confess that we invented the end to the story – that they were compiling an accommodation guide for the Gay Cyclist Club of Great Britain and they wanted to include The Angler's Retreat in the Club Guide on account of the great welcome Billy had extended. This gave us an hilarious hour in the boat, while we tested Billy's reaction to the possibility of regular parties of lycra-clad riders arriving every summer and expecting a special welcome from Billy.

That night as a joke I tied up some pink, pearl and pale blue wet flies. Derek and I named them Billy's Fancy as a reminder of a fishless but fun day in the boat. To my great surprise the pattern has turned out to be very effective for both trout and sea trout. I have also tried them on America's West Coast rivers and they are great for summer Pacific Salmon and Steelhead! The original pattern was tied as a tandem (another part of the same joke). *Taken from an article in US magazine West Coast Fly Fishing and Tying Journal, Autumn 1998.*

BILLY'S FANCY
Hook Wet fly 10 or 12 thread white **Tail** Small bunch magenta pink bleached and dyed squirrel tail **Body** Medium pearl mylar **Wing** As tail tied so that the tip of the wing ends over the tip of the tail **Hackle** Dyed light blue cock saddle fibres, tied as beard, long enough to cloak hook bend **Over-wing** Two strands pearl or silver flashabou

---

John & Felicity Bartleet
Essex

Hospitality and Guidance! Those two words sum up Billy and Marion. We like to think of ourselves as regulars, though we have only stayed three times at The Angler's Retreat. Always a huge welcome from Marion offering refreshment the minute we step through the door. Putting the world to rights over dinner; hearing all the local news from Billy; then, 'Right, what do you guys want to do?' Our week is planned with enthusiasm and skill . . . a day on Loch Bee with Billy . . . John gets a six pound sea trout on Loch Fada . . . The days flash by.

John's Favourite Uist Flies

STOAT'S TAIL

Hook Size 4-12 doubles or trebles **Thread** Black
Body Black rayon silk **Tail** Golden Pheasant crest
Tag Fine silver tinsel **Rib** Medium oval silver tinsel
Wing Dyed black squirrel tail hair
Hackle Black cock hackle fibres.

George Campbell & Bill Cook
Ayrshire

First Impressions

Having fished our way all around Scotland, including Orkney, Lewis and Harris over many years, we were based in North Uist in 1998. Being of an age that appreciates outboard engines, which are not allowed on North Uist, and short hikes to waiting boats, we invariably found ourselves travelling to fish in South Uist.

After a poor day on Loch East Bee we met a then unknown 'well dressed' cockney angler who was about to go fishing. Billy introduced himself, enquired where we were staying (mentioning that he ran The Angler's Retreat) and freely offered advice. Unaware of his long residence in South Uist, we took his advice with a little reservation, especially when he then produced a spinning rod and electronic fish finder from his car. Apparent confirmation of not being the type of fishing that we had in mind, the double positive, unique to Scotland, of 'Aye right' came to mind.

However, being tolerant sons of Old Scotia, we did book our stay with Billy and Marion for 1999 and we have been satisfied regulars at The Angler's Retreat ever since. It was during our second stay with Billy when he innocently and casually mentioned the large pollack that inhabit Loch East Bee. He said he had confirmed their presence by means of expeditions to the loch with fish finder and spinning tackle following reports by anglers of having hooks straightened, or of being broken out by big fish.

All finally became clear, particularly as by then we had learned to appreciate Billy's extensive, expert knowledge and skill as a fellow fly-fishing angler. First impressions can be misleading, sometimes.

George with two Uist trout.

Bedspreads and National Flags

We arrived as usual in 2006, a football World Cup year.

Marion, after welcoming us, announced that she and Billy had specially decorated the downstairs single room in which Bill would, as usual, be staying. She was keen to show Bill the result.

Bill followed Marion into the room whereupon he discovered to his horror that the bedspread and matching pillowcase were in the style of the English flag, the St George's Cross. Various comments flowed before Bill finally regained his composure, and some of his national Scottish pride.

Marion explained afterwards that the bedspread was actually for her grandson. The room now sports a tartan bedspread and pillow case.

Editors' note: Marion adds that, having bought the St George's flag bedspread for their grandson, she and Billy decided to play this joke on Bill. They knew Bill was not exactly a keen supporter of the English national football team which, unlike Scotland's, was competing in the World Cup that year. The resulting comments which 'flowed' from Bill were unrepeatable in a family publication like this.

Bill's Favourite Uist Fly

THE PROFESSOR
Hook size 12/10 **Thread** Brown **Body** Primrose yellow floss (off-yellow) **Tail** Red hackle barbs or 3 long Red Ibis fibres **Hackle** Ginger cock **Wing** Mottled grey mallard **Rib** Gold oval tinsel

George's Favourite Uist Fly

BLACK CROW
Hook Various, but mainly Grey Shadow, size 10 **Thread** Black silk **Tail** Claret pheasant tail or black cock hackle fibres **Hackle** Equal number of red and black hackles, palmered to give a big bushy bob fly
I got my first Black Crow from Billy. Fished on the bob, it has been very successful for me. I tie it very bushy as my philosophy regarding flies is 'to let the b******s see it.'

Brian Concannon
Dorset

East Bee

As a keen fly fisherman who lived on the Uists for eleven years while serving in the army, I had many memorable fishing experiences there. Since moving back to the mainland, I have returned to the Uists every year to enjoy the fishing and the wonderful hospitality of Marion and Billy. It was on two of these annual visits that I experienced the two best fishing days of my life. On both occasions I was fishing with Billy.

On one visit I elected to take a South Uist Estate rod for salmon and sea trout fishing and go on the Lochboisdale Hotel roster for the various lochs. This was arranged by Billy who was also the ghillie for a great friend of his who was staying at the hotel without a fishing partner. Billy had arranged for me to partner his friend. The Estate then owned the hotel and ran the fishing on estate lochs through its fishing manager John Kennedy.

At the beginning of each week the fishing manager would draw up a roster on which the hotel guests were allocated the lochs which they would fish each day. The intention was to give everyone a fair chance of fishing the 'best' lochs. During this period Billy was one of the official ghillies who could be called upon by the fishing manager. Guests staying in the hotel had priority on the roster, but if there were lochs not in use by hotel residents then anybody else could fish, paying the fishing, boat and ghillie costs.

One of the days we were allocated Mill Loch. Mill had not been fishing well so we agreed after consultation with Billy that we should go elsewhere and we chose Loch East Bee. I had fished that loch many times over the years and, as many anglers will agree, the fishing is always unpredictable. On

Brian and Bo out sea fishing.

this day it was absolutely right for me. The weather was overcast with a light westerly wind giving only a slight ripple on the water. We fished along the east side of the main, or top, part of the loch and I started taking spectacular, hard fighting, wild Loch Bee brown trout. Altogether I landed seven trout between 2.5lbs and 3.75lbs, four of which were over 3lbs. All these wonderful trout were taken on my own tying of a Green French Partridge, size 10, on the top dropper. This made the experience even more memorable, and all because we decided to go to East Bee rather than Mill!

Lower Kildonan

On a subsequent visit, late in the season, Billy had arranged to fish another one of the estate sea trout and salmon lochs, Loch Lower Kildonan. Our ghillie was a local man who was on the list of experienced ghillies run by the estate fishing manager. On this occasion we agreed that we should all take turns at fishing and managing the boat. It was blowing half a gale with substantial waves on the loch requiring skilful control of the boat along the eastern shore in the strong westerly wind.

When we were fishing into one of the many bays on the eastern shore I hooked what I thought was part of one of the numerous bits of old barbed wire fence which are found below the surface of the water there, just as Billy and our companion were changing places in the boat. These are not the ideal conditions in which to hook a fish but it was indeed a fish as I discovered when 'the fence' started moving out into the loch. The 'ghillie', having taken his seat, started to row the boat into the middle of the loch. Doing so was no mean achievement in such a strong wind and I recall Billy saying afterwards that he was pleased he didn't have to do it himself. Anyone who knows how strong an oarsman Billy is will appreciate how wild the wind was that day.

I knew it was a heavy and powerful fish, but once we were in the middle of the loch I was able to take control of it. Even so, at one point Billy turned his face away because the rod was bent over so much he thought it was going to break. About 20 minutes after that the fish, a salmon, jumped clear of the water, showing its size and causing me to ease up on the pressure I was putting it under to try to tire it out before bringing it to the net. When I did eventually get it into the boat the fish weighed 15lbs, which was a very good size for the Uists and another memorable fish, and day, for me. The fly, again, was a Green French Partridge, size 10, fished on the top dropper.

Brian's Favourite Uist Fly

GREEN FRENCH PARTRIDGE

(Ted Dunn's pattern) **Hook** Standard wet trout, round bend, down eye, size 10 **Thread** Pearsall's dark green silk
Tail Golden pheasant crest **Body** Dark green seal's fur
Head hackle French partridge breast feather in front with stiff, dyed dark green cock hackle behind it.

This Irish mayfly pattern was brought to the Uists in the early 1980s by Ted Dunn when he became an agricultural advisor for the North of Scotland College of Agriculture at Balivanich on Benbecula. It is a priority fly for the Uists. When fished wet, ie spent, it is excellent for salmon, sea trout and brown trout.

Charlie Cox & Nigel Houldsworth

Perthshire & Roxburghshire

Fishing With Billy

A is for Arrival at The Angler's Retreat

B is for Billy always gung-ho to meet

C is for Comfort and Charlie, no tackle as usual,

D is for Dinners always met with approval

E is for Exhaustion after days on the go

F is for Fada, and Fankles, but go with the flow

G is for the Garage stuffed full of tools old and mod

H is for Houldsworth's renowned gift with his rod

I is for 'Ideal' wind, and huge rollers to match

J is for Jinxed, but a plan next year we'll hatch

K is for Kildonan, conditions perfect for sure!

L is for loud Laughter, but the fish they stay dour

M is for Marion's meals – was it haddock or hake?

N is for 'Not again, Charlie, DON'T STRIKE FOR GAWD's SAKE!'

O is for Oh for a fighting sea trout on the line

P is for Billy's 'relief' Pot tipped into the brine

Q is for Quality – the best 'hol' by a mile!

R is for the Raj and B & M's trips there in style

S is for Stories, a mix of old, tall and true

T is for Too much to repeat, mostly Too blue

U is for Uist, its scenery sublime

V is for Vast contrast with London's 'leaves on the line'

W is for all the Wonderful times that we had

X is for the EXtreme kindness shown to us lads

Y is for 'Your Good Health', years and years to enjoy

Z is for Zillions and Zillions of thanks from us boys.

Nigel with two salmon from the Bharp sea pools, caught within minutes of each other at the end of a tough, wet day.

Nigel's Favourite Uist Fly

WILLIE GUN

Hook Size 10 doubles or trebles **Mount** Waddington shanks, sizes 2.5-7.5cm **Thread** Black **Body** Black rayon floss **Rib** Flat gold tinsel **Wing** Black, orange and yellow bucktail. *I use quite a lot of gold flashabou to make the fly pulsate in the water as it is retrieved. I have caught a number of salmon in the sea pools below Loch Bharp with this dressing.*

Matthew Crampton

London

Salmon Fishing

It was early in my trips to Uist, and early in my learning to fish, when flushed from landing my first decent trout and thinking I might just be getting the hang of this loch-style angling, I thought I'd try my hand at fishing for salmon.

My motives? Well, ticking a box, I suppose, so I could say I had tried it. Pushing myself to learn new skills. Plus – to be honest – part of me wanted to expose the myth that catching these silver fish was exciting enough to warrant the greater expense and tedium.

So some months later, on a blowy day in late September, I found myself heaving an outboard over the stile that guards the boat station on Loch Bharp. I'd somehow persuaded my cousin Tim to join me; a regular of Cuba, Florida and Chew Magna – and near full time angler – he was the closest thing to a fishing guru in my acquaintance. Captaining the boat was the esteemed David Peutherer, who felt the conditions were pretty good. A further presence in the boat, as always on Uist, were the words of Billy Felton; particularly his warning after breakfast that day: 'Whatever you do, don't strike too soon.'

When embarking on new pursuits, I tend to be fuelled more by anxiety than enthusiasm. So it was this morning. I was scared. My only consolation was the thought that it was unlikely any of us – especially me – would actually make contact with a salmon. So I determined just to stay calm and concentrate on my casting.

We motored up to the top end of the loch where the wind allowed a steady drift down the Northeastern shore. David was on the oars, Tim at the back and I, fortunately casting over my right shoulder, was up at the front. I carefully followed instructions to cast within inches of the shore, between the outlying boulders. Scared of snagging those rocks with the unaccustomed weight of a huge Bibio double on the point, my first casts fell safely short then came closer. After a few casts I did catch a rock, but it came off easily, then I caught another one, again it came off, and no longer did I worry.

After a while I actually started to relax. This salmon business wasn't too hard. All I had to do was cast like this for a year or so, then maybe I might get a fish. It was a relief that the challenge was within my grasp, while the loch was so pleasant that I didn't mind bobbing around for a day without result. We had reached a famous mark called the Elephant Rock and I spent a few moments trying to configure some elephant in its shape.

Having attained this calmness, just ten minutes into my first ever day of salmon fishing, I snagged my Bibio again. This time, however, it didn't come off. Instead it started pulling. Well, I thought, there's plenty of trout in this loch, so it's no surprise I have hooked one. This was quite a firm pull. 'I think I'm on,' I muttered to my companions, 'Could be a nice brownie.'

At which point a grey submarine – not your little u-boat, but a huge, massive nuclear jobbie – shot straight out of the water, curled to its right and smashed back through the surface. My line went slack. 'Ah,' said David. 'That was your fish of a lifetime.' I barely heard him as I sat shaking at the front of the boat.

My line was cleanly broken. The consensus among the experts was that I was unlucky: that the salmon, trapped in shallow water, had jumped straightaway and perhaps landed on the line, but certainly shattered it in the initial surge of escape. I shook as I reeled in. I shook as we talked about it. I continued to shake for 15 minutes. Something serious had changed. Fishing was no longer the schoolboy prank of pulling wriggly things out of the water. For the first time I'd made contact with something stronger than me. And that, I assume, is what salmon fishing is about.

Losing it

The way you fish reveals the way you handle the other sex. Or so claimed a friend of mine who's never resorted to marriage, probably because he's been practising Catch and Release for too long.

One evening on Uist I recalled that same friend asking – is it better to have hooked and lost than never to have hooked at all? Yes of course, we thought at the time. Being able to hook them, even if they get away, is surely better than not being able to hook them at all. But what about the pain when they stop pulling – that sudden ache when they escape you and you're left alone? Well, yes, that's bad, but surely worthwhile…

It was an evening in late May. I'd spent several days trying to cast through a near-unfishable gale and felt as battered as the bushes. But now the wind had steadied into a sweet southwesterly. Marion's dinner had made everything feel possible again. And there were still some hours before sunset.

I pondered where to head. For no particular reason I thought of Cille Bhanain, a loch I did not know well. 'Watch out,' said Billy, 'there are some big fish in there.' Good, I thought, it's about time for me to catch something decent.

Two chums had departed the day before, smiles on their cheeks and the whiff of several three pounders upon their landing nets. I, on the other hand, had had an embarrassing run of losing fish. One solid brownie had profited from a poorly tied knot, my inadequacy evident from the pigtail end of the returning dropper. Another got away when the hook split

straight through the shank, though I won't blame myself for that as I was testing, during teabreak, a friend's fancy Sage set-up.

The third great escape was entirely my own fault. I was wading East Bee by the small causeway. I cast into the slack pocket behind a protruding rock. There was a vicious boil at my muddler. The line broke straightaway. It was only four pound line, foolishly left on after an untypical tiddler session

One day Matthew will learn how to hold a fish when being photographed.

earlier that day. For years Billy had told me never to go less than six pound on Uist. Why do we always have to suffer before we learn?

So, mindful of these failures and my friends' successes, but buoyed by the good conditions, I headed for Cille Bhanain. It's an unlikely spot for leviathans, being little more than a large puddle. Even when the water's high you seldom go out of depth, though be careful testing this as the bottom's often sticky.

I got there just before nine and spent longer than usual on knots. I set up my standard Uist rig of Soldier Palmer Muddler on the point and a ginked up Loch Ordie on the bob. The wind was angled perfectly for covering good water. I started by the well preserved building on the dun – another oddity of this loch – and made my way back along the deepest channel of the loch.

Evening is my favourite time to fish, especially if I've already fished all day. It feels like bonus time. Somehow this releases me from the humming expectation that lines my daytime effort. I cover water more methodically. I expect less.

By now I had worked my way round the rocks beside the dun and was casting out into mid stream between them and the far shore. No fish were making their presence known on the loch, certainly not near my fly, and I sensed nothing to support Billy's claim of big fish. But then again, you seldom see Uist fish before catching them.

And then, quite out of the blue, I hooked the largest trout I'd ever seen alive. I knew this because it immediately jumped high above the water. In case I hadn't seen it clearly enough, it jumped again, and again, six times indeed. And each time my heart jumped with it, for so often I'd lost fish during just such leaps.

But the fish stayed on. And now it shot over to the reeds on the other side of the loch, some forty yards away and well into my backing line. Again my heart went with it, for so often I'd lost fish during just such runs.

And as my heart lurched, my head reeled from the mental cocktail of playing a good fish – a measure of nerves, a glug of glee and a dash of machismo, all laced with two fingers of imminent doom. Yet the fish stayed on.

I played it off the reel, twisting fast the handle, frightened I could not retrieve swiftly enough to maintain pressure when it swam towards me. And I saw it again, once as it jumped, then for longer as it patrolled the water just beyond my reach. And I was thinking the myriad thoughts you do. Why aren't my mates here to see it? Thank God they're not. Will those knots hold? Will the hooking survive another jump? Will the loose bobfly snag on a reed? Can I handle losing another fish? Does my future fishing depend on this moment? Will success mean I'm a hero? Will failure mean I should give up?

The tragic thoughts we cram into those moments.

By now the fish had taken three runs and still I had control. It was idling closer than before, almost within reach, perhaps even tired. For the first time I felt confident enough to reach behind my neck for the net, releasing it with the same blind fumble that always finally works, while my rod hand stretched ever higher above my head. And at this point, for the first time in the fight, my mood swung from doom to hope. Okay, his head's not yet up so I'll keep the net away from the water, but surely he's safely hooked, knackered and soon will be mine. And then, sweet Jesus, I'll have beaten my bad luck. I'll be one of the boys. I'll be a proper fisherman.

The trout must have read my thoughts. He turned slowly, well within reach, then ran once again. This time he ran more fiercely than before, and within seconds the leader had snapped. It was over.

I retrieved the line and consoled myself it wasn't my tying that had lost the fish. I sat down on the rocks, lay down the rod, and wept. The loss felt very great. More than simply the loss of one fish, albeit a magnificent one, it sealed a run of luck so foul – so hopeless – that surely I should quit this painful pastime.

Just then the sun peeped out for one last, low glint. I looked around and felt the full recuperative blast of a Hebridean sunset. Maybe it was the light, maybe the tears, but I suddenly felt better than I had in days. Of course it was better to lose fish than not fish at all. What's important is not catching fish, or even hooking them, but the steady, repeated returning to the water. Whatever the conditions, whatever your recent record of failure, just keep putting the hours in. And if you're really cut out for this painful pastime, then you'll find strange reserves of hope coming to meet you at the start of each day's fishing.

A Day on Bee

And what is the quintessential South Uist fishing experience? For many it is a day on a machair loch and, yes, there is little to surpass the joys of fishing such fertile, shallow jewels.

But I would argue that the loch which best embraces the qualities of this island is East Loch Bee. Here you will find all you need. There's a full array of fishing feature, from sandy to gravelly bottoms, shallow flats to deep pools, narrow cuts to vast open drifts, islands, weedbeds and skerries galore, along with miles of glorious rocky bank. There are hill lochs to feed it and a sea channel to drain it. There are hills alongside, Ruabhal, Beinn Tarbert and the harshly named Hecla, which provide rare topographical feature in such flat terrain. There's birdlife, amazing birdlife, enough to make even a determined non-twitcher such as myself ask to borrow the binoculars. And the fish, ah well, I'll come to the fish later.

On the map East Bee resembles the lower reaches of gastric anatomy, albeit with some strange colonic backwaters. This complex shape is its glory. Wherever the wind blows, at whatever strength, and however cold or sunny the air, somewhere on the loch will suit the conditions. Such variety does not guarantee fish, my goodness no, but it does give you choice. And with Uist's wild weather, such choice gives anglers their vital fix of hope.

Yet East Bee is not to everyone's satisfaction, as you'll find in Bruce Sandison's story 'Useless on Uist' elsewhere in this book. Many treat the loch like an attractive but unlikely date – they're happy to step out with someone so gorgeous, but don't expect anything to come of it. I've blanked there more often, when fishing primarily from a boat, than even the machair lochs. But when Bee does put out, boy does she give you some action.

Her trout are the 'hard men' of Uist. They punch well above their weight, so a savage take seizing line from your hands may reveal a fish of barely three quarters of a pound. They usually weigh in heavier than that, just above a pound or so, and like patient muggers who wait before pouncing, they'll follow your fly right up to the boat before grabbing at the dibble. In fact they like to chase, so we tend to cast a longer line on Bee just to give them the pleasure. And there are many, many fish of two, three pounds and more – so, given their vicious takes, you'd be a fool to sport leader of less than six pound strength.

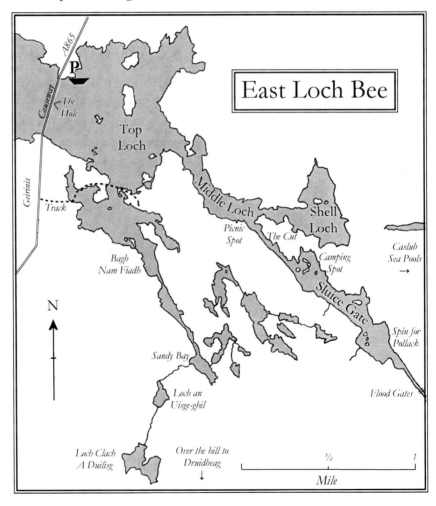

Hard they may be, but Bee trout are also pretty boys. Lovely and golden, sometimes quite green, always muscular. And being a brackish loch (don't forget to rinse your tackle boys when you get home from this date) you may encounter sea fish.

Overall, the loch's a stunner who often breaks your heart. But if you stay at The Angler's Retreat and you're lucky enough to fish with Billy, then one factor outweighs all others. She is, quite simply, Billy's favourite loch. Given the choice, he will always come back to Bee. However she treats him, he'll book the boat once again. And even when you stand before him, fishing log in hand, and you detail the percentage of blanks on the loch then, through denial, loyalty or whatever, he'll calmly ignore your figures and suggest once again 'A Day on Bee'. Through his persistence, I've come to share his love of the loch.

Let me recount then, a typical day on East Bee. It starts easily, with a five minute drive south from The Angler's Retreat to the large loch carpark (itself a rarity on Uist). From there you can see how the weather's hitting the main expanse of the water and so create an initial shape for the day. With the boat baled and kitted out, ends allocated for those two fishing first, and ghillying quotas settled (usually thirty minutes apiece), the wind may let you drift straight off from the boat station.

If so, you may soon find yourself over the Hole. This deep pool extends barely ten yards out from the single channel through the road causeway from West Bee. It is a place of legend. Not only huge trout, but sea trout, small salmon, pollack, saithe, herring and smelt have all appeared here. Once Brian Concannon and Billy's son Fraser had a bag full of mackerel. One visitor, an early riser, religiously attends it each dawn by parking nearby and wading up to its fringe. His daily ten minute communion (five minutes each side of the causeway) bears much excitement over the course of a week, including much breakage as hooked fish often swim through the pipe under the road. Personally, I've moved a couple of fish there but hooked nothing; and fishing it separately smacks of shooting fish in a barrel. But I'm always happy to drift over it.

Your first few drifts take you across the open loch which, far from shore and flat of feature, may appear pointless. And often is. But it's all shallow and weedy, there are fish there, and sometimes you rise them. You then spend some time around the islands and skerries. This is as exposed as you get on this loch so, if the Uist wind is blowing its usual hooley, this makes for some exciting ghillying. Whatever the direction, you can usually steer the boat past a succession of rocky possibilities. If these prove promising, you might spend the whole morning in this area. More likely, you'll soon move on to Middle Loch.

Here, your passage depends on the season and water level. As the year progresses, thick weed chokes up most of the narrow loch. If the water's low, and the weed high, then your engine will stutter through what appears a green vermicelli soup. But if the water's high, or it's late in the season, then you can fish the top eighteen inches of clear water down this central channel – that is, so long as you're fishing a floating line and large, surface-hugging flies. Which you should be, as they tend to deliver the most fish on this loch.

The prime stretch of Middle Loch – the narrow, weed-free strip hugging the rocky north shore – can be fished at any time. Its rocks and indentations make most inviting water. It should keep you busy through the rest of the morning so, by one o-clock when you remember your hunger, you point the boat over to the south shore, just west of the Cut through to the Sluice Gate. Here another ritual awaits. Once the boat is pulled ashore, all fishermen strip off their coats and waistcoats, then peel down their waders to relieve bladders. Should anyone go some distance and turn away to perform this task, Billy will scorn such shyness and turn pointedly towards the group. Be warned, this sight may put you off your sandwiches.

Loch-side picnics are always a pleasure. They're usually the first chance to relax after a morning of unbroken concentration. We fish hard in the boat, squeezing every cast out of every drift, keeping fly changes to a minimum and staying constantly focused to avoid fankles. Lunch lets you slow down. Even if it's raining hard, you sit content within the amphibious cocoon of chest waders and waterproof jacket. You gobble and gossip. You sip warm coffee. You watch the loch.

After a while, as others kip, someone peels off to put a few casts down the Cut. This narrow deep channel screams fish, and sometimes delivers them. After a morning crouched in the boat, your body loves standing to cast. There's plenty of wadable water around the picnic spot. Gradually the group starts fishing again, each relishing the freedom of casting alone. But if the fish don't rise, then it's back to the boat for the afternoon's schedule.

Usually this means a short motor through to Shell Loch. Chug gently as, to enter this part of Bee, you must skirt some sharp, sub-surface sentinels. But once arrived, you feel you have entered an enchanted place. A hundred swans will slowly fly off, like wartime bombers vacating an airfield – and almost as noisy. Unseen other creatures will no doubt be watching you. Around you is a rugged, anvil-shaped loch, whose shores and islands suit any wind, but demand attentive hands on the oars. There's soft, sandy wading on the northeast shore. Shell Loch can produce fish when all other parts of Bee have failed. You can also, if the tide's right, park the boat and hike east to the Caslub seapools. So much choice, so little time…

By late afternoon it's time to head back. Someone starts the engine and you settle into a magical half hour ride home, reflecting on the day, discovering that forgotten chocolate bar from the packed lunch and, like some great explorer, perusing the passing vista and wildlife. You traverse the narrows of Middle Loch then the open hugeness of the main loch. You unpack the boat, uppack the car and head home to rest limbs and eat dinner.

And later that evening you come back out again. Some people can settle down to watch the news or the football during the long Hebridean twilight. I can't. And often I return to Bee, this time taking the track opposite Geirinis down to the small causeway that bisects the southeastern arm of the loch. Here you enter wading nirvana – acres of waist-deep, weedy, sandy-bottomed water, punctuated with boulders, framed with rocky shores. After a day spent cooped within a boat, it's delicious to wander at will. And these evening sessions tend to be more productive than the day – the only problem being how to store the fish you keep. I'm not a creel kind of guy, so I end up with a bass bag tied to my wading belt and slapping against my thigh.

When it's nearly dark, try a few casts in the floodplain nearer to the road. Here, in water barely a foot deep, you can find fat trout taking supper in the shallows. A one and a half pounder once grabbed a fly at my feet when the water barely covered my boots. He must have been the village idiot.

You take a final cast. Then a final, final cast – and just one more, why not. But now it's too dark to retie flies and you've felt a windknot near the point and, well, that's decided it. No more fishing today.

But tomorrow you could return to Bee and fish a whole day without touching any of the water I've mentioned. Walk across the hill from Druidibeg, fish the hill lochs then work your way up the southeastern arm. Or take the boat through the Cut to the Sluice Gate, with its deep pool where you can spin for large pollack, then hike past the floodgates to fill your spare bass bag with mussels…

It's this variety that symbolises Bee. She's the Desert Island Loch, the place I'd choose if forced to fish one loch for eternity.

Matthew's Favourite South Uist Flies

SOLDIER PALMER MUDDLER

I don't have a tying recipe as I do not tie my own flies. Mostly I use a cheap lot of Soldier Palmer Muddlers bought from an itinerant tackle seller in a church hall in Portree. One of these 45p flies took a 3.5lber, a 3lber and a 2.5lber off West Ollay during a recent day in September. I only take this muddler off my point on Uist if it's sunny or calm, or I'm trying for a sea trout.

LOCH ORDIE

I've bought or borrowed many versions of this fly. All seem to work fine, ginked heavily and dibbled religiously on the bob. Graham Gauld describes a Loch Ordie dressing later in this book.

Edward Evans

County Antrim

First Sea Trout

I was introduced to fishing in South Uist many years ago. Coming from Northern Ireland I did not know what to expect but, having heard about the great fishing, I was tempted to go. Alistair Scott, head gamekeeper on the island, arranged for me to stay with Marion and Billy at The Angler's Retreat.

After a very short time it was as if I had known them all my life. I was made so welcome. Indeed we became such good friends that in 2006 I had the great pleasure of accompanying them on their annual visit to India, something which for me was the trip of a lifetime. The Angler's Retreat is a unique place and will be sadly missed when Marion and Billy finally give it up.

Marion is a lovely, generous person who makes everyone welcome. And the food, well that is something else. I usually have to diet before and after my visit. From a good healthy breakfast through packed lunches to a fantastic dinner, everything is prepared and cooked with the utmost care. And of course, after dinner a wonderful day of fishing is often finished with Billy's stories around the table. So many, so funny and all so interesting.

For Billy, who came from London, it is unbelievable the wealth of knowledge he has about all aspects of fishing. He seems to know every loch on South Uist. Everything is so carefully planned for every guest for each day, probably due to his army background. Weather forecast, choice of lochs, type of tackle

Edward on Stilligarry.

75

and flies, directions etc. All is done with military precision.

I have never had a day's fishing on South Uist on which I did not catch fish and this is mostly due to Billy's knowledge and expertise. A day's fishing with Billy on his favourite Loch East Bee is something that will always be remembered. I treasure these memories, especially the times when I was able to have my son Alwyn with me. He gained so much from the whole experience.

Billy's trophy board, on which he displays photographs of guests with their best fish, is proof of his ability to point fishermen in the right direction and it is an honour to have a few photographs on it. It is enough to say how good things are, when so many fishing guests return year after year.

One of my most memorable days was fishing Mill, which is one of the salmon and sea trout lochs, with Billy and Hamish. Fishing for sea trout was something I had never done before. To catch several, the best of which was five and a half pounds, and lose one which was undoubtedly much larger, was another unforgettable experience of my association with The Angler's Retreat and the beautiful island of South Uist.

Edward's Favourite Uist Flies

CONNEMARA BLACK
Hook Size 10 **Thread** Black **Tag** Orange floss
Tail Golden pheasant **Rib** Fine oval silver tinsel
Body Black seal's fur **Wing** Bronze mallard
Hackle Black cock hackle with a few fibres of blue jay

CLARET BUMBLE
Hook Size 10 **Thread** black **Tail** Golden pheasant tippets
Rib Fine oval gold tinsel **Body** Claret seal's fur
Body hackle Black and claret cock hackles
Collar hackle Blue jay or dyed guinea fowl

THE BLACK CROW
see Ken Arfield / George Campbell

David Fullerton

Inverclyde

Wind Up on Altabrug

I have had several memorable days on Loch Altabrug, in typical Uist weather: howling gales and pouring rain!

On both visits to South Uist I was in a party of either five or six friends, this allowing us to split into two groups and fish several different lochs on the one day. On my second visit I fished Altabrug with Steve Martin, Paul Smith, Alan Mooney and Frank Struthers. We had a very successful day, mostly on the Olive Bumble, Clan Chief and Lough Arrow Mayfly.

Later in the day I was fishing on the small island/peninsula nearest to the house beside the loch, and was catching a fish more or less every cast when I met Paul. He was making his way back to the car. When I spoke to him, I discovered this was because he had fallen in the loch and was soaking wet. This caused great hilarity amongst ourselves, particularly Frank who can never resist a good wind up and proceeded to crack every funny ever written about drowning, and then said he wished he had brought his video camera from the car. This prompted him to get it and use it to film some footage of myself catching the free rising trout from the island.

After a short filming session Frank decided to wade across the bay to get a closer shot. I remarked that he had better watch his footing or he would be emulating Paul's earlier effort. No sooner had I said it than Frank proceeded to fall head first into the loch, complete with video camera in hand. He surfaced coughing and spluttering with smoke and sparks spouting from the camcorder. Talk about speaking too soon! The incident caused further great hilarity at the dinner table that night, where it was commonplace to swap fishy stories and the occasional shaggy dog one.

Predicament on Stilligarry

In May 2005 Alan Mooney and myself had a session on Loch Stilligarry, on a perfect evening. When we arrived at the loch we met a French gentleman who, if memory serves me correctly, was married to a Californian lady. They were in a bit of distress as, returning to their car after a day's fishing, they found it half submerged in mud, for they had parked it beside the track to the loch. Myself and Alan, who have probably forty stone of 'muscle' (ha, ha) between us, made light work of their predicament and their antiquated Mercedes was soon back on a firm footing.

Afterwards the four of us had some great chat, swapped fly patterns and enjoyed the general companionship that exists amongst trout anglers. The evening then proceeded to produce some excellent trout for Alan and I and ended with a beautiful sunset.

Druim an Iasgair

On one occasion we fished a small trout loch called Druim an Iasgair. This was during our first visit to South Uist. I still have the entries in my fishing record book to this day. The loch housed nets belonging to a fish farm and Billy had told us there had been a little accident involving a few farmed sea trout being released into the loch. But it was our first night on South Uist and Billy assured us it would be a good start to our holiday.

On arrival at the loch we saw several large sea trout heading and tailing on the surface. After covering a number of these fish with lure type patterns with no success I changed to a couple of palmers, namely an Invicta Bumble and a Blue Zulu. After one or two casts the Blue Zulu was

swallowed by a fine sea trout which, although hardly a natural fish, gave a tremendous account of itself.

When landed it weighed three and a half pounds, a fine start to what was to be a fine holiday. This incident proved Billy's unerring ability to put his guests exactly where the fish are. The fish also won me the prize for heaviest fish

David '20 stone of muscle' Fullerton.

of the holiday, despite the fact that

David Ballantyne landed one of two and a half pounds from Loch East Bee during the same week.

Putting on the Glad Rags

Most of my other recollections relate to drinking exploits, the consequences of which there were many.

During one week we saw posters advertising a disco at the Greagorry Hotel. We decided to pay this a visit and arrived with great aplomb and without doubt overdressed for the occasion. This became apparent when, on entering the premises before the disco started, we were greeted with people wearing boiler suits, wellies and lumberjack shirts. It was a local shindig indeed.

Despite being overdressed and drawing some strange glances from the locals, we soon entered into the spirit of things and joined in the mayhem. When we asked the barman where the disco was, he enlightened us to the fact the juke box was on free vend, ie there was no charge for playing numbers, and the disco didn't start till later. After a few shandies we were informed the bar was closing and there would be entertainment in the hall next door. To our dismay we found when we went in to the hall that we could no longer purchase any of the amber nectar and had to make do with what we had, only to find that the locals, being aware of this situation, had stocked up with pints of whisky, vodka and other suitable refreshments. This is where the glad rags came into their own as we attracted the attention of the local talent who were only too keen to share their beverages with us.

It turned into an excellent evening and showed just how welcoming the locals are to complete strangers. Several of us went back to The Angler's Retreat early that evening leaving the budding Casanovas to it. At the breakfast table next morning, whilst tucking into another of Marion's marvellous breakfasts, we were soon being given a run down of the previous night's exploits from those who stayed late. The main topic was a romantic interlude with a lovely young lady whose name I will not mention as it was somewhat unusual. It did however lead to a challenge being issued to all at the table to see how many girls' names we could think of ending in 'ina'. We came up with a few and were reliably informed a few more existed on the island. It was an hilarious start to another terrific day.

Oysters or Scallops?

One evening we were tucking into a prawn cocktail starter, professionally prepared by Marion. This led to a discussion about the merits of shellfish and after much discussion most people decided their favourite was either oysters or scallops. This discussion was followed after dinner by another drinking session, this time in the Black Island Hotel on Benbecula.

Once again we were received splendidly by the locals and later in the evening were informed by Frank that he had arranged to meet a chap next day in relation to getting some shellfish. At breakfast next morning Frank announced that he wasn't going to fish and would instead go for a hair of the dog and to find out if the local chap was a man of his word.

After another wonderful day of fishing we met Frank back at The Angler's Retreat, slightly worse for wear but sitting proud as punch with a sackful of scallops. These had been produced earlier by the chap from the hostelry. Much to the delight of six hungry mouths, who soon demolished them, they were superbly prepared by Marion for our evening meal.

How Billy can sample her excellent cuisine every day and not be as wide as the gable end of their house remains a mystery to me. Anyone without the chance to sample Marion's lovely cuisine is a poorer man for it.

David's Favourite Uist Flies

CLAN CHIEF
Hook Sizes 12, 10, 8 standard wet fly **Tail** Red over yellow floss
Body Black seal's fur **Rib** Fine silver wire **Hackle** Red & black
cock wound together, palmer fashion
Front Hackle Black hen, slightly longer than body hackles
*Editors' note: The original Clan Chief was created by
John Kennedy, fishing manager for the South Uist Estate.*

WHITE HACKLED INVICTA
Hook Sizes 10-12 **Tying Silk** Brown **Rib** Fine oval gold
Tail Golden pheasant topping **Body** Yellow seal's fur
Hackle Ginger cock palmered **Wing** Hen pheasant
Front Hackle Long white cock

Graeme Gauld

Aberdeenshire

The Boys from Aberdeen

For many years a group of four friends – Graeme Gauld, Bob Adams, Iain Low and Davie Adams – travelled far and wide on fishing adventures from Orkney to England, Sutherland to Ireland, but nothing prepared them for what lay ahead in the strange island of South Uist.

Ever since a youngster Graeme had aspired to fish the world-renowned machair lochs, his life's ambition being to catch a wild brownie of three pounds or more. With this in mind, during the summer of 2004 Graeme started planning the group's first trip to South Uist. After many phone calls and e-mails, Graeme proposed that the group stay with Billy Felton at The Angler's Retreat Guest House. Everyone agreed and started thumbing through John Kennedy's book *70 Lochs*, enabling Graeme to organize the trip and book boats with the precision of a military assault. The group then turned to fly selection. Between them, they only had around eight thousand flies to choose from – which would obviously not suffice for a new venue. So they talked some more, bought some more and tied some more. Meanwhile Graeme kept in constant contact with Billy to ensure that everything was OK. On all previous ventures, they'd ensured the boat confirmations were cast in stone before they booked the accommodation. This was not the case with South Uist, where boats only get allocated at the start of each week. Billy kept telling Graeme not to worry, the boats would be fine. Graeme, who had not yet experienced personally the weight of Felton Reliability, kept worrying.

Given their usual trick of getting lost on new trips, the group decided to leave Aberdeenshire very early so they could arrive at the ferry terminal with time to spare. But on this occasion things went so well the group reached Uig three and a half hours early for the ferry (not bad as it only takes four hours to drive there from Aberdeenshire). This ensured pole position not only in the ferry queue, but also in the petrol station, the café for bacon sandwiches, the bar and the pool table – all important when trying to compensate for spare time which could better have been spent in bed.

The group proceeded to board the ferry. This was not Graeme's favourite part of the trip as he gets chronically sick in any sea greater than a flat calm. But he was prepared to make this personal sacrifice for the good of the group and the fishing trip, though he was not prepared to make this sacrifice quietly. After an agony of closed eyes and deep breaths (not that he was complaining), the group disembarked and made the journey from Lochmaddy to The Angler's Retreat where they received a hearty welcome from Billy and Marion. This included what was to become a tradition of tea and cheese scones (which, so soon after a ferry journey, tend to make Graeme chuck up, but are much appreciated by the others).Thence the group took off to reconnoitre the lochs on offer. Back to The Angler's Retreat for dinner and to find out their boat allocation for the week. Graeme need not have worried as Billy had managed to secure everything that had been requested. The group then settled into their regular post-dinner antic of playing cribbage (or as Billy calls it 'Fifteen-Two, Fifteen-Four and One for his Nobs'), drinking beer and forcing down copious amounts of port.

The boys from Aberdeen.

The following morning the group sat down to a hearty breakfast, only to look out the window and be met with the sight of horizontal snow – not the best of weather conditions for their first fishing day on South Uist and more than a bit unexpected on the 15th of May. Out to the car with all the paraphernalia and off to East Loch Bee (Billy's favourite). Billy was to accompany them on the first day and would fish with Graeme and Bob in the morning and Iain and Davie in the afternoon. It was at this point they found out why Billy had recommended they bring waders – all the boats were in three feet of water. Being the great host that he is, Billy waded out and got the boats for those in the group who had only turned up with wellies. With the boats kitted out, discussions were held as to the best fishing locations and Iain and Davie took off to the Islands while Graeme and Bob started a drift along the Causeway with Billy working as their ghillie.

Billy set up the drift and in the process swapped seating positions in the boat with Bob. Meanwhile Graeme took the opportunity to start stripping line and casting in the traditional loch style. Billy not knowing the angling ability of his guests – and probably accustomed to new visitors who could not fish over the front of a drifting boat – asked Bob to pass him his rod. Billy proceeded to show Bob how to fish by starting his cast and saying 'just do what Graeme is doing'.

This was like a red rag to a bull. Bob and Graeme have had years of friendly challenge as to who will be top rod on the day. Billy's instruction was met with a retort from Bob saying 'I've been fishing for Brown Trout for 25 years, don't f***ing tell me what to do! Give me my f***ing rod back!' Billy took this well, handed back the rod and continued to ghillie for the rest of the morning like a gentleman. Graeme was however unsettled and feared the trip might be marred by the incident. But he should not have worried as Billy, with years of experience of dealing with people, waited for the right moment one evening and dropped it into conversation. Everyone had a good laugh. To this day it remains a standing joke whenever the group gets together.

The weather was against the group that week. Even so, everyone enjoyed their stay, caught their share of fish, and lost some lunkers – even if Graeme failed to realize his ambition of catching a three pound trout. Hooked by Billy and Marion's hospitality and generosity, the group booked their next year's trip on the spot. After a fond farewell, the lads left the Anglers

Retreat once again with plenty of time to reach their ferry. This time it was just as well as they managed to miss the turning to Lochmaddy. Fortunately all roads on North Uist seem to lead to the port, so they still made the ferry with time to spare.

Next year they returned. And each year after that. And Graeme caught his first three pounder on Stilligarry. Now he's chasing a four pounder...

Graeme's Favourite Uist Fly

LOCH ORDIE

Hook Size 8 longshank **Tying Thread** Orange **Rib** Oval tinsel
Tail 2 dark red game tied hackle point, approx. length of hook
shank **Rear Hackle** 2-3 dark red game (soft cock hackles)
2nd Rear Hackle 2-3 medium red game (soft cock hackles)
3rd Rear Hackle 2-3 light red game (soft cock hackles)
Front Hackle Ginger (soft cock hackles) **Head Hackle** 2-3
turns of white hen. Quantities of hackles to suit
preferred hackle density.
*We like the Loch Ordie very much as it can be used to great effect on the top
dropper, at various sizes on any type of wave. It probably accounts for 80%
of our brown trout, no matter what loch we are fishing.*

Bill Green
Surrey

Carrots or Worms

20TH MAY 2003. The four of us – Bill, Dave, Derek & Franco (The 'Italian Stallion') – were sitting socialising with a little after dinner whisky. Derek, who had pulled a muscle falling into a peat 'hole', was asking Billy what the fishing was like on the loch at the bottom of the garden, which I believe is called Loch an Os.

Billy said the loch was not very good for trout but had large eels and a few pike. Derek asked what bait he would suggest and was told that worms would be best. Billy gave Derek a torch and suggested he go round the side of the house and kick over the compost patch as it was usually full of worms. Derek appeared twenty minutes or so later and said, 'I can't find any bloody worms', which surprised Billy & Marion who said there were always worms there.

The next day, on returning from our day's fishing, we were met by Billy standing with his hands on hips looking furious. 'I spent all day yesterday digging, tilling and planting a vegetable patch with neat rows of carrots, lettuce and so on – and some idiot has kicked and trampled the whole area!'

Derek blamed the whisky.

Editors' note: The whisky may have impaired Bill's hearing as there are no pike in Loch an Os, but there are some very large trout – one of which rests proud and stuffed on the wall of the dining room at The Angler's Retreat.

John's Whisky

One year we allowed our friend John to join us. He had pestered to come along on hearing our tales of wild fishing, wild places, good company and good food. He was told that part of the requirement to join our group was that he had to bring a bottle of single malt as the four of us are whisky fans. John is only an occasional whisky drinker but, being in business, had a good stock of special malt whiskies which he had received over the years from business contacts.

On arriving back to The Angler's Retreat after our first day fishing, the first thing we usually did was to drink a dram to the day. We were sitting in the upstairs lounge when John plonked his bottle on the table and said he was going for a shower. We couldn't believe it – the malt was in an individually numbered bottle, from a single cask and 25 years old, so very, very special and expensive. We opened the bottle with reverence and for the next 40 minutes or so we 'oohed' and 'aahed' and went into raptures over this super special whisky.

When John appeared – all fresh, showered and changed – he asked 'Was the whisky OK?'. We pointed to the empty bottle. We'd enjoyed it so much we hadn't even saved him a taste.

Friends eh?

Bill's Favourite Uist Flies

My favourite two-fly cast for fishing the Uist lochs is a Black Pennell on the point and a Claret Bumble on the dropper.

BLACK PENNELL
Hook Kamasan B170 size 10 or 12 **Thread** Black Uni 8/0
Head Bead Red glass 2.3mm **Tail** Golden pheasant tippets
Rib Oval silver **Body** Black floss **Hackle** Black cock tied long
I use the standard tying, but I put a small red glass bead on the hook, up against the eye, before the normal tying. I whip off behind the bead. This significantly improves the fish appeal of the fly – probably because the little extra weight at the eye makes it move a little differently.

CLARET BUMBLE
Hook Kamasan B175 size 10 or 12 **Thread** Black Uni 8/0
Rib Oval gold **Tail** Golden pheasant tippets
Body Claret seal's fur (or SLF dubbing)
Hackle Black & claret cock palmered together
Shoulder Hackle Blue jay (or guinea fowl dyed blue)

Robert Hannah

Ayrshire

The Piercing

This incident happened a few years ago during a stormy day on Loch Fada while I was on one of my regular annual visits to The Angler's Retreat. It must put me in line for the heaviest 'catch' on record on South Uist.

Billy and David Peutherer were ghillying that week for three anglers who were salmon and sea trout fishing on the estate lochs. One of them, Olivier, was French and a guest of the other two. I think he was their business client. I am mainly a trout fisherman but one day Olivier very kindly invited me to join him for a day on Fada. I happily accepted. David was our ghillie.

Although the weather was stormy the conditions looked quite good and we were hopeful of getting a fish. However, after fishing for an hour or two during which we made no contact with any fish, and as far as I remember didn't see any either, I decided to try a big double as my tail fly. If memory serves me right it was a Teal Blue and Silver. If not that then it was something equally colourful. Everything went well to start with but, during one particularly heavy and unexpected gust of wind, I managed to accurately hook Olivier just above the eye with the fly. Fortunately he had very fleshy eyelids and no serious harm was done.

As I didn't want to remove the hook from such a delicate place while we were in the boat in stormy conditions, we offered Olivier the option of going ashore and being taken to a doctor to have the hook removed. He would have none of it as he said it would interfere with his fishing. My only option was to use an 'elastoplast' to tape his eye wide open until lunch time, when the situation could be re-assessed. Olivier fished on for the rest of the morning.

Fada is one of the lochs which has a fisherman's hut and, over lunch there, we met up with that well known ophthalmic surgeon Billy Felton. During his many years fishing and ghillying, Billy has probably seen just about everything that can happen to a fisherman. He took one look at the hook before producing an old pair of pliers from one of his pockets. Then, very calmly, he held Olivier's head still, used the pliers to flatten the barbs, gripped the hook in the pliers and, with a very professional looking flick of his wrist, pulled out the double hook. Olivier didn't even flinch. The whole 'operation' took only a few seconds and allowed him to fish for the rest of the day, which he did with great determination but sadly no success. I don't think he ever came back to South Uist, but I am sure this wasn't because of the quality of the 'medical' treatment which he received.

Patient and Opthalmic Surgeon seem on reasonably good terms after removal of double hook from eyelid.

One other thing happened in the hut. In Olivier's eyelid the fly looked like one of those piercings which some youngsters have in their noses, ears and other places, except that the hook was much more colourful than the gold of which they are usually made. On seeing it in his eyelid someone in the hut, I really can't remember who, said it looked so nice that Olivier should consider getting a matching one in his ear! Thinking about it now, I am surprised no-one asked him for the fly which Billy had removed, since it was the only one which caught anything that day.

Small Loch, Surprisingly Big Fish

The following year I was out fishing some of the lochs near Stoneybridge with Billy. One of them I had fished before and I knew Billy had also fished it several times. While we were there, I happened to mention a smaller loch just on the other side of the track used to access the area. It was narrow enough to be able to cast easily from one side to the other. Billy said that in all his years on the island he had never fished it and suggested I give it a try. The next day was the last of my holiday so I decided to take his advice by fishing it and some other lochs.

I arrived back at The Angler's Retreat at tea time, woke Billy from his Saturday afternoon siesta and asked him to come out to the jeep to view my catch. You should have seen his face – there were three fish of 1lb 8ozs, 2lbs and a superb 4lbs 10ozs. I had caught the largest one in that little loch. It was a wonderful end to my holiday and proved the value of two pieces of advice for anyone fishing on South Uist: always take the Master's advice and always be willing to try some lochs you haven't fished before.

Robert's Favourite Uist Flies

DETACHED FOAM-BODIED DADDY
Hook Size 12 **Body** Black foam **Legs** 6 black, knotted pheasant tail fibres **Hackle** Greenwells (cock)

RED TAILED MUDDLER
Hook Size 10 **Body** Silver Lurex **Rib** Medium silver wire **Tail** Red wool **Head** Spun brown deer hair

---

Bob Hutchinson

County Clare

Fishing Lessons

The first time I went to South Uist the weather was terrible. In fact it was so bad that, had it not been been for the help and kindness I received from Marion and Billy, I would not have gone back.

It was on that first trip that I discovered Billy takes the matter of boat handling very seriously, irrespective of who is on the oars. One day when he and I went fishing we drove to the loch in his Suzuki jeep, rather than in my car. This resulted in me leaving my sunglasses behind. As luck would have it, it was a very sunny day. At one point, when I was on the oars, I was supposed to be positioning the boat so that Billy could fish along the edge of a weed bed, keeping it just the right distance from the weeds. He kept complaining that the boat was either too near the weeds or too far away from them, never in the right place. He was right of course. What I didn't like to tell him was that because I was looking right into the blazing sun without my sunglasses, I couldn't see clearly where the reed bed was! Lesson one: don't forget your sunglasses.

Lunchtime at West Olavat - Billy & Bob contemplate defeat in the Olavat Challenge.

On another day when I went to Hallan with my friend Allan the rain was absolutely lashing down. We filled the outboard engine with petrol and put our waders on in the garage before we left the house. Unfortunately we didn't make sure the cap for the engine's petrol tank was on tight enough. Consequently petrol spilled out and we had to spend valuable time cleaning out the boot rather than fishing. Lesson two: always check the petrol cap BEFORE you put the engine in the boot.

Anyway we had our day on Hallan, at the end of which I took my waders off and, as I didn't want to walk on the wet grass in my socks, asked Allan to put them in the boot for me. Unfortunately he didn't hear me and the waders were left lying beside the loch. Of course we only discovered this when we arrived back at The Angler's Retreat and so had to go all the way back to the loch to get them. When we got there we couldn't find them where we were sure they had been left. It took us a few moments to see where they were – floating away across the surface of the loch. We had to take the boat out again to retrieve them. Lesson three: if you are going to leave your waders lying about where they can be washed on to the loch buy the same make as mine – Dry Feather. They float!

Bob's Favourite Uist Fly

LADY ETHNA
Tag Glo-brite Green No.12 **Tail** Pure white
Body Silver with copper wire rib **Wing** A few fibres from
Grey Mallard Flank feather, four strands of Pearl Krystal
Flash, white fibres from a childrens' dressing up wig
Hackle White cock swept back **Head** Red
Editors' note: Bob ties the flies sold at The Angler's Retreat, which are used and greatly appreciated by many guests. His own favourite, tied on size 12, 14 and 16 singles and trebles, is the Lady Ethna - a salmon fly which is also successful for trout. Bob originally tied it for use in Connemara but has also used it, on size 8 and 6 hooks, for salmon in Canada. Unusually, part of the wing is made from material used in making novelty wigs children wear for dressing up at Hallowe'en. This adds new meaning to the expression 'dressing a fly'.

Pete Matthews

Leicestershire

20-plus Summers on the Uists

My friendship with Billy, Marion and their boys goes back over 25 years. From 1981 to 1987 I was Boys' Games Teacher at St. John's Prep School, Alton, Staffordshire, which Billy's three sons all attended. I taught his two youngest sons, Gavin and Fraser, who were both very talented at sports, and still are. I later came to know Billy's eldest son, Danny, very well, fishing with him on many occasions. I've always loved Scotland and I've spent many happy summer holidays fishing on the mainland. Towards the end of my time at St. John's, Billy was posted to the Hebrides. His youngest son, Fraser, had always been enthusiastic about fishing and is today an accomplished fly fisherman. Knowing I had fished for many years on the west coast of Scotland, Fraser suggested I pay a visit to the Uists. That summer myself, my brother Dave, and another friend Bucko, did just that, pitching our tents on Alan and Katie Buchanan's camp site at Shell Bay on Benbecula. Since then, I've returned to the Hebrides for over 20 years, usually spending five to six weeks exploring the fisherman's paradise which is the Uists. Over that period, I have fished with Billy on probably over 100 occasions and lived to tell the tale, despite the vagaries of his casting! But I must pay tribute to Billy, and to Brian Concannon, who over the years helped me to learn so much about fishing on South Uist and Benbecula.

Wanderings with Bo

For years Billy and Marion had a most wonderful Jack Russell, known as Bo. She was mad keen on fishing, whether from boat or bank. Whenever we went boat fishing, Bo always sat on the ghillie's seat, staring intently at the water, watching for the slightest sign of a rise or a follow. Her concentration put her human colleagues to shame. She had very little time for anyone who failed to connect with a take, whereupon she would give you a look of total

Bo near Bee.

disdain, telling you exactly what she thought about your lack of fishing ability. Fellow anglers who have shared a boat with Bo will know what I mean.

Billy spent a lot of time ghillying during the summer months and I would often call round and pick up Bo from his house. I really enjoy walking out to the lochs on South Uist and Benbecula which are away from the road, many of which never get fished from one year to the next. Bo walked miles and miles with me over the years and she had endless energy. If I fell asleep in the heather after lunch, she would always wake me up with a lick of my face, as if to say, 'Come on Pete, there's thousands of trout out there and you're not going to catch them like that!' She's now buried on an island on East Bee, where she no doubt appreciates being surrounded by all those trout and watching Billy go past on the outboard.

Crickets on Bee

East Bee has a special place in my heart and anyone who has spent time exploring this great water will understand why. It's also Billy's favourite loch, I'm sure, and I've spent hundreds of hours fishing it with him, in all weathers and conditions. On one occasion in the late 1980s Billy was enthusing about the great sport he'd been having, dapping with live crickets, and asked did I want to join him? I asked him where the crickets were and he said, 'in the car'. This proved to be very accurate indeed, as he had left the lid off the container. We proceeded to spend over an hour gathering the crickets from inside the ashtray, under the seats, on the carpets and everywhere else in the car. I'm sure I wasn't the only person to spend time valeting his car as, whenever I crossed the causeway between East and West Bee, there was always Billy to be seen, dapping away. Towards the end of the summer, Billy was back using traditional loch-style methods. He claimed those were most effective for that time of the season, but I'm convinced that the change of method was only because Marion had given him the all-clear regarding the car!

The Gap in the Causeway on Castle Loch

I'm sure Billy will forgive me telling this story, but anyone who knows him well will also know that that he is very rarely wrong with his opinions. Anyway, one day Billy, Brian Concannon and myself were sharing a boat on Castle Loch, with Bo sniffing the air at the front (she was often a canine figurehead when we moved on the outboard). Brian has a vast experience of fishing on the Uists and as we motored out from the boat station, the conversation went something like this:

BRIAN: 'We ought to start in the West Bay, the other side of Castle Island and work our way back on the wind.'

BILLY: 'Yes, I was thinking that, too.'

BRIAN: 'Billy, you're too close to the south shore, you can't get through the gap below the island, as there's a causeway just below the water.'

BILLY: 'I know, but there's a narrow gap, just wide enough to get the boat through; I went through it on the outboard a few weeks ago.'

BRIAN: 'You're wrong, Billy.' (Not always the right thing to say to Billy.) 'You can't get through.'

Billy then proceeded to rev up the outboard to its maximum speed, heading straight for the supposed narrow gap. I was sitting in the bow, watching and listening to the two experts, wondering which one was correct. I began to get a rough idea when Brian emptied his pipe, put it away, then adopted a brace position, holding on to his seat with a grip of iron. I looked over the bow and saw the causeway racing towards us at an astonishing rate of knots, so I followed Brian's example and I, too, adopted the brace position. We hit the rocks with an almighty crash, finishing about four feet out of the water, wedged firmly on the causeway. Bo, in the bow, was the only occupant of the boat who did actually get into the West Bay. The poor dog, oblivious to the discussions in the boat, was catapulted through the air for about 40 feet before landing in the loch on the other side of the causeway. She swam back to us, jumped into the boat and showered us with spray. Nobody said anything for what seemed like an eternity, until Brian filled his pipe, lit it, and said, 'Shall we go back and around the other side of the island now, Billy?' Of course, Billy could not possibly be mistaken. He replied, 'Yes, we'll have to. It's amazing how much the loch has dropped during this fortnight of dry weather.'

Billy and Marion

On a more serious note, I would like to thank Billy and Marion for so much over the past 20 years. They probably felt I was a bit mad, spending six weeks in a tent with whatever the Hebridean weather can throw at you. I've accepted many invitations to share Marion's wonderful cooking, usually at weekends, and her curries are infinitely better than the ones I usually had out of a tin can. Also, it's very difficult to do a full roast dinner in a tent! Billy has been so unselfish in sharing his experience with his guests and he has always found time to help anyone who shares his love of fishing and the Hebrides. I've been very lucky over the years and I've fished with him on all the classic lochs of Roag, Fada, Kildonan, Mill, Bharp etc, together with the famous machair lochs of Bornish, Grogarry, Stilligarry, West Ollay and others. East Bee remains my favourite, though, even if the fishing is a little harder these days.

For several years Billy talked me into doing a few days ghillying when John Kennedy was short of a ghillie – and he would always give me a thorough briefing if I was on a loch I didn't know too well. Afterwards, we would often fish together in the evening, when the hotel guests had finished for the day. Deep down, I know that Billy loves his wild brown trout fishing, as I do. One day we had both been ghillying – Billy on Roag and myself on Lower Kildonan – and we had agreed to meet up later and fish together on whichever loch we felt had the best prospects. Billy finished first and drove down to me at Kildonan (remember, this was before mobile phones.) We had both had really hard days, with light winds and a bright sun. Roag or Lower Kildonan: which of these famous salmon & sea trout lochs should we fish? We looked at each other, then simultaneously looked over the causeway at the inviting empty boat on Upper, rather than Lower, Kildonan. An evening with its obliging brown trout was much more tempting than going over and over the waters we had been flogging unsuccessfully all day. I'm not sure how many other anglers would have made the same choice, but we elected to go for the brown trout. We had a great evening's sport on Upper Kildonan with the brownies and, as we watched the sun set in the west, there was no finer place in the world to be.

Pete's Favourite Flies

Soldier Palmer is my Number One and I've probably caught more two pound-plus trout on it than any other (six off East Bee in one season alone). **Kate McClaren, Claret Bumble, Ke-He, Black Pennell** are also top flies. **Bibio** is tops when heather flies are out from about mid-August. **French Partridge** is very good in a big wave. Try a **Mini-Muddler** on the point and you might get a red-letter day in July, sometimes in bright sunshine. **Butcher** or **Teal, Blue & Silver** are also top flies on the point, especially in brackish lochs where bigger trout feed a lot on fry.

Alan Mooney

Inverclyde

Meeting Bruce Sandison

I stayed with Billy and Marion on three occasions and each time they were on hand with a warm welcome and provided us anglers with a 'home from home' on our fishing trips to South Uist. Marion's wonderful home cooking kept our 'army' marching on its stomach and Billy's willingness to ensure our fishing trip was fulfilling was tireless. His knowledge of the islands and wildlife, together with his organisational skills, even down to giving us detailed daily local weather information, was invaluable. Billy also took time to fish with us and the knowledge which he shared will stay with us for a very long time.

We always looked forward to Marion's home cooked evening meals after a hard day's fishing – her venison lasagne was renowned, that was of course after the delicious pickled trout sandwich and other items which she provided for our packed lunches. Her home-baking was also a firm favourite. Many plans for late evening fishing trips were abandoned after Marion's dinner!

On such occasions the company in the house never disappointed. It was a pleasure to dine with like-minded people, swapping anecdotes and sharing knowledge.

One of my most memorable trips to The Angler's Retreat was when I sat at the dinner table with the man whom I most admire in the angling world – Bruce Sandison. I have followed Bruce's works through radio and I have read many of his books on angling and hill-walking. Imagine my delight to be in such a man's company!

Bruce is passionate about Scotland's national heritage and actively campaigns against the salmon farming industry and the effect it is having on Scotland's wild places and native species. It was such a pleasure to dine with a person holding such knowledge, which he was so willing to share with us, a man who is passionate about his country. Bruce fascinated us with tales of his many trips around the world and shared with us some of his experiences – a night not to be forgotten. One of my most treasured possessions is a card signed by Bruce.

I have travelled extensively in Scotland and stayed in many establishments, many of which were considerably more costly, but none of these have provided the quality of service experienced at The Angler's Retreat. I could not imagine a better place to unwind and lose the stresses and strains of every day life. It was always a sad time when you had to pack up your things and return to reality.

Alan's Favourite Uist Flies

YELLOW & ORANGE 'STRADDLEBUG'
(Stan Headley's pattern) **Hook** Sizes 8-10 **Tying Silk** Red
Tail 5-6 cock pheasant tail fibres **Body Hackle** Hot orange hen
Rib Medium oval gold **Head Hackle** French Partridge

LOUGH ARROW MAYFLY
(Frankie McPhillp's pattern) **Hook** size 8, B175
Tying Silk Brown **Rib** Fine oval gold
Tail 3 fibres cock pheasant tail **Body** Natural raffia
Hackle Short Badger Cock with French Partridge
dyed green drake in front; Grey Partridge dyed yellow
in front of the French Partridge
*I have successfully fished these as a two-fly cast
on a slow intermediate line.*

James Paterson

Roxburghshire

Billy & the Mobile Phone

I believe it is widely known that Mr Felton is very careful with his money. I wouldn't say tight, but careful.

This story is aged by the fact that it dates back to when mobiles were very rare and expensive. The only places in South Uist where a signal was available were at the car park at Loch East Bee and the bottom of the track after Grogarry House. The phones resembled half bricks and had a very limited stand-by time but amazing street cred.

Billy was not convinced about the value of having one because of the limited use, plus the cost of the calls. He thought it was mental to pay 25/30p per minute plus £15 per month to do something which could be easily accomplished for no cost on his landline after he had finished his duties for the day.

As matters progressed, mobile coverage began to spread over the island but he steadfastly refused to buy a mobile phone purely because of the cost. Apparently, my phone was rubbish as one of his guests could receive a signal in the part of East Bee known as Shell whereas my phone lost the signal after you left the main part of the loch. I was apparently wasting my money and I should buy an identical phone to this particular guest.

Eventually, Billy bought Marion a pay-as-you-go phone because it was cheap. This was not the smartest thing he has ever accomplished. The pay-as-you-go phone needs to be charged after the requisite phone time has been used. One problem for William was that there was nowhere on the island to top up your phone at that time. He then evolved a complex operation where one of his guests would take the phone to the mainland, have it charged and sent back by mail. He was unconvinced that the spent phone was valueless despite many hours of argument.

The big day came when we were fishing Fada and he announced that he was getting a 'proper' phone which didn't need to be topped up and this phone had amazing coverage especially in South Uist, so the salesman had guaranteed. Furthermore, his phone was much better and cheaper than my phone as he didn't have to pay any line rental for six months and the calls were only ten pence a minute. The calls would be debited to his business bank account.

I said, 'You have given them your bank account number?'

'Yes, of course – how else would they collect their money?' Billy replied.

'You do know that they will contact your bank for a reference?'

'No, but I have an excellent relationship with the bank and the bank manager, so that will present no problem.'

'H'mm, how do you feel about the £30 opinion fee the bank will charge?' I asked him.

A pregnant silence followed by a stream of oaths then, 'They can't do that – I haven't told the bank they can.'

'You should look at the small print. Ask Jonathan.' Jonathan, my son, told him that at the end of the day he would be £30 down. Another silence and then another stream of oaths – 'Can I borrow your phone?' he says.

'That'll be £30 to use it then,' I cheerfully replied.

More curses as I gave him the phone which he couldn't work. As regular punters know, Fada is in a hollow and the mobile phone coverage is not that good. So back to the boat station at maximum speed. Much leaping out

of the boat and scurrying to the top of the bank where he eventually gets through to the Bank of Scotland.

Back he comes, 'Right, you pair of bas****s, the bank tells me that under normal circumstances, they would charge £30 but on the basis that I am such a good customer, any fee would be waived. Satisfied are we?'

James Paterson in his prime.

'Actually, we thought that as (a)

TALES FROM THE ANGLER'S RETREAT

we have saved you £30 for something you don't really want and (b) we have wasted the best part of an hour of our fishing time whilst you farted about with the Bank of Scotland, you wouldn't make a charge for ghillying for us today!' we said. The reply is unprintable.

Billy the Surfer Dude

It would probably be the late 80s/early 90s, when Mr Felton started to ghillie for us just after he left the army.

This particular week my son Jeremy and I had managed to get Loch East Bee for three out of our six days. At that time Bee was regarded as an enigmatic loch, sometimes good but mostly difficult. Billy knows more about Bee and its moods than any one else. It is my favourite loch on South Uist as you never know what you might catch (a stickleback or a salmon). This was in the days of the Lochboisdale Hotel which at that time was in its full glory.

Regulars to South Uist will know that the sun is an absolute killer with or without the wind. Unless you screen up, your face tends to become very tender after a couple of days. At that time proper fishing sunscreen and lip balm were very difficult to source and obviously impossible to get on South Uist. Billy's lips were like Jubes Jubes,* plus being very tender and sore. Jeremy and I were using Zinc Oxide lifted straight from the repertoire of American/Australian surfers which came in such colours as Shocking Pink, Brilliant Blue and Blinding White. It acts as a total sun block and also makes you look cool!! On applying this, Billy remarked that we looked like a couple of 'shirt lifters' to which I replied that maybe so but at least (a) we didn't have sore lips, (b) we didn't look like a 'white darkie' and (c) we could eat hot curry with impunity. Billy couldn't eat anything hot because of the state of his lips. Billy loves his food, especially Indian curries.

Wednesday came and we were asked by Billy about the state of our lips to which I replied that they were fine as the Zinc Oxide totally blocks the sun. Billy's lips were in a pretty bad state and he had resorted to rubbing them with suntan lotion which not only comes off easily but tastes hellish (so he tells me!!).

Lunch time came around and he asked to see the Zinca (Zinc Oxide) which comes in a little plastic container.

'So this stuff really works then?' was the cry.

'Of course it does as long as you don't mind looking like a shirt lifter,' was the response.

'I was a Sergeant Major in the Army and I couldn't risk my reputation being seen with this stuff on my choppers,' Billy said.

'Fair enough then William, you'll just have to sit there and suffer for your reputation.' I believe he used several profanities at this point, which I could not repeat here.

That night he suffered badly for his reputation and I believe his usual sunny disposition was affected by being unable to sleep because of his lips.

Next day as we headed up the first drift, he asked if he could use some of the Zinca as his lips were very painful. I deliberately gave him the Shocking Pink. As he looked very like the Joker in 'The Dark Knight', Jeremy and I fell about the boat with laughter.

'So there'll be no use of cameras allowed today then?' we said, which was met with another stream of profanities. You need to remember that, at that time, there were no digital cameras otherwise I would have a photograph to this day.

'Listen you two b£%*&rds, especially you Paterson, not a word of this to anyone – understand? I spent over 30 years building up a reputation as a hard man in the army. If any of my squaddies saw me now, my reputation would be totally shot.'

The Zinca worked its magic and, every morning before the first drift, he would apply another violent shade to his choppers and on the Saturday he could even eat Marion's curry without any pain.

Billy & Jeremy on a day when cameras were allowed.

I offered him the three tubs at the close of play on the Saturday but these were declined on the basis that, if anyone else saw him, he could not be sure that his application of coloured substances to his lips would not be interpreted in the wrong way.

And yes, we caught loads of fish, thanks to Billy.

Jubes Jubes are an old style Scottish Sweetie, shaped like lips a la Michael Philip Jagger.

James' Favourite Uist Flies

HEAVY PETER

Hook Size 10 or 12 low water salmon doubles which have 'a bit of length' **Tail** Fiery red (scarlet ibis or plain cheap hen hackles dyed bright red) **Body** Either gold or silver holographic tinsel wrapped over with gold or silver wire to protect the tinsel – use holographic because it seems to give better flash than the normal flat tinsel **Head** Two hen hackles for softness, wound two or three times; black head cement

The Heavy Peter originated from a fly called the Wee Peter which was first tied by a solicitor from Skye. In designing it he pirated an Orkney fly called The Priest, which proves that there are no new flies, only thousands of variations on a theme. The fly is basically a Bloody Butcher tied with a head hackle rather than a wing, fished on the point. If you prefer a single hook, tie flattened lead wire onto the shank to weight the hook and take it down. That's why this is called the Heavy Peter rather than the Wee Peter.

BILLY BONDS

Hook Partridge GRS12ST – grey Shadow Emerger/Nymph, sizes 10 and 12 (probably size 10 for salmon and sea trout, size 12 for brown trout) **Tail** A bunch of claret pulled from a hen cape. **Body** Blue or even pink holographic tinsel protected by silver wire; the hackle is made of three feathers, either two blue and one claret or two claret and one blue, tied bumble style to achieve a mix of colours down the shank and tied off with the silver wire to secure it. **Head** Two blue or claret cock cape feathers; black cement

Very appropriately – since Billy Felton is a West Ham supporter – this fly is named after an all-action midfielder who played professional football for West Ham United and was idolised by their fans. The fly is tied in the team's colours of claret and blue, and is fished on the bob. The reasons for the specific choice of hook are a) it doesn't rust and b) the hook has an upturned eye which holds the fly in the correct alignment as it is retrieved across the water.

David Peutherer

Glasgow

Make Yourself Comfortable Over There

F ive words etched forever in my memory.

A few years ago, while I was staying at The Angler's Retreat, Billy wanted someone to keep him company when he went shooting. I had never been interested in shooting but knowing how much Billy enjoys it, and always being ready for a new experience, I offered to go with him one evening.

We set out in the jeep not long before dark, complete with gun, dog and, in my case, about six layers of clothing including my neoprene waders. Our destination, I thought, was the machair west of Loch West Bee. So it was, initially, but only in the sense that the machair was where Billy parked the jeep before heading off at considerable speed on foot towards the loch. My efforts to keep up and avoid losing sight of him in the increasing darkness were made more difficult, first, by all the layers of clothing which severely restricted my movement and, second, by the fact that the machair was crossed every fifty metres or so by wide drainage ditches of uncertain depth. These were the kind of ditches which have clumps of grass and weeds on the surface which you can never be sure will take your weight if you stand on them. Billy crossed the ditches with the confidence which years of experience and his detailed knowledge of the machair had given him, and with hardly any loss of speed. I entered them nervously, waded across very gingerly half expecting to sink beneath the surface with every step I took and, because of the tightness of my waders, struggled to get back out on the opposite side.

It was with considerable and breathless relief that I reached the loch shore which I thought must surely be our final destination. I was wrong again. Billy and dog went straight into the loch. I could hardly see where I was going and had no idea how deep the water was ahead of me. I made sure that I followed exactly the same route as Billy. A few minutes later – maybe it was seconds but it seemed like minutes – we arrived at a small island which at its highest point would have been less than a metre above the level of the loch. In the centre there was an old, partly collapsed gun butt surrounded by mud or, to be more precise, cold, wet mud. Billy sat down on the shore of the island with his feet in the water and the dog behind him. Pointing towards the mud he said, 'Make yourself comfortable over there.' Comfortable? Sitting on cold mud in the dark! I wasn't lost for words. Plenty came to mind, none of them complimentary. I said nothing.

Billy shot, if I remember correctly, one duck that night. The dog retrieved it from the loch. I know because I heard the shot and then the dog in the water. How either Billy or the dog saw the duck I have no idea. I saw absolutely nothing, or at least nothing with feathers and wings. All I saw was a faint light in the sky to the west and the dark silhouettes of Billy, his gun pointing skywards, and the dog.

That evening did not give me a desire to take up shooting. But it did give me an appreciation of the beauty of the machair on a calm night, the dunes silhouetted against the sky, the moonlight reflected on the surface of the loch, the silence and the stillness.

And A Black Bird Sang

The first few times I went to South Uist I spent almost as many days looking at archaeological sites as fishing. On one occasion I went to Usinish on the east side of the island to look for a group of souterrains. These are thought to have been built during the Iron Age about 2000 years ago, and were probably used for storing food. In most places they were built underground but where, as at Usinish, there was insufficient depth of soil they were built on top of the ground. I had once crawled into a very wet underground one on Skye but had never seen one on the surface.

The easiest way to go would have been to follow the path round the coast from Loch Sgiopoirt. I decided to go via the top of Hecla, starting from Loch Sgiopoirt, striking out across the moors then climbing the shoulder which stretches north from the top of the hill.

It was a beautiful spring day. The walk up the ridge was easy. My enjoyment of it being only slightly spoiled when I was overtaken and left far behind by a couple who looked at least twenty years older than me, but greatly enhanced by seeing a golden plover. It must have had eggs or young nearby. It ran away from me zig-zagging from side to side, stopping and starting, dragging one wing on the ground as if it was broken, tempting me to follow it. An oscar-deserving performance from a beautiful bird.

The view from the top was breathtaking. From Mingulay to Harris, the Outer Hebrides lay spread out before me and for the first time I could appreciate how much of South Uist is covered by lochs. Then, typical of the early season weather on the island, a black cloud came over. For about twenty minutes I sat on top of the hill with my knees close to my chest, my waterproof jacket pulled down over my knees and legs and my head bent down inside the hood, battered by hailstones.

The descent was one of the most unpleasant I have ever made. On the east side of the hill the peat was saturated. With every step my boots sank deep into it. Soon they were full of water and, to make things worse, it was soaking up the legs of the trousers I had on under my waterproofs. I was almost wishing I had gone the easy way. But then the sun came out again and in front of me was Usinish and to the south of it Loch Coradail, a loch which I had not and have still not fished.

I quickened my pace, sploshing along as the ground became firmer, then stopped when a deer suddenly appeared no more than a hundred metres in

front of me. At first I thought it must have been lying in the heather and stood up when it heard me or caught my scent. But I hadn't noticed a low cliff in front of me. When I got closer to the top of it I saw that the deer was one of a group of eight hinds which had been grazing out of my sight near the bottom of the cliff. When they saw me they lifted their heads and looked at me then slowly turned

David impersonates George Formby with a three and a half pounder from West Ollay.

106

and trotted away. There are so many deer in parts of Scotland now that it is easy to become blasé about seeing them. But to see them in the wild like that is still for me a special experience.

When I got to the bottom of the hill to my surprise and delight I quickly found the souterrains. Rectangular, about three or four metres long and one and a half metres wide with low stone walls and corbelled roofs, one was partly collapsed but both were in remarkably good condition considering their age.

Nearby I knew there were, but couldn't find, the remains of a hut circle, a round stone house in which the people who built the souterrains had possibly lived. On higher ground to the east, I could see a cairn built about 6000 years ago by Neolithic farmers as a place in which to bury their dead and at which to pay respects to their ancestors. I went down and stood on the beach where they would have first landed on the island and from where they would have set out to fish in the sea. For a while I stood there thinking about their way of life – keeping some sheep and cattle, growing crops in small fields, fishing, hunting, living in thatched houses – and how little it differed until very recently from the lives of the crofters on South Uist.

Heading north I passed but didn't stop to visit the remains of some old shielings. Until about the middle of the 19th century people would have lived in them during the summer while their animals grazed on the same pastures which the animals of the Neolithic farmers had grazed thousands of years earlier. Further evidence of continuity. Sheltered from the west wind by Hecla the walk was easy but very warm. By the time I got near the coast at the east end of Loch Sgiopoirt I was hot, tired, hungry and getting worried that I might be late for dinner. And then something happened to which had it been on the mainland I would probably not have paid any attention.

Away to my left there was a rowan tree growing out of a crack in a big rock. It was the only tree I could see in the whole area, and on it there was a blackbird, and it was singing. I stood and listened to it. I could almost imagine it was singing 'Look at me, I'm in a tree' or maybe 'I'm the king of the tree'. Being Spring it probably had other things on its mind. Whatever it was, it provided me with a perfect end to a wonderful day.

The Eagle Has Landed

Lots of people who visit Scotland go home thinking they have seen a golden eagle. They are more likely to have seen a buzzard. Apart from birdwatchers who know the difference, most people are unable to distinguish between buzzards and eagles because they only see the latter at a great distance, usually high in the sky. Having spent many years hill walking and fishing in the highlands and islands of Scotland, South Uist in my experience is the one place where there is a good chance of seeing golden eagles close up – and two of the best spots are the middle and eastern parts of East Bee.

East Bee, mid loch, three men in a boat. Billy and Hamish fishing, me on the oars, terrified of allowing the boat to diverge from its course and correct angle to the wind by so much as one degree lest I am accused of neglecting my duties. Or, to put it another way, working hard to hold the boat at just the right angle and distance from the shore while they faff about catching nothing in perfectly good fishing water to which I have brought them with supreme skill. Aye right!

We were no more than a hundred and fifty metres from the north shore where a bank about ten metres high slopes steeply down to the water, when Billy spotted a golden eagle. I looked up and saw it flying low above the bank. I watched it as it flew eastwards then slowly swooped down below the top of the bank where, to my amazement, it landed on a big rock and stood there in the classic picture postcard pose – its body sideways on but its head turned towards us. I could see the details of the feathers on its body, its talons gripping the rock, its powerful hooked beak and dark-looking, piercing eyes with which it seemed to be looking straight at us with no semblance whatsoever of fear. I watched it for a few minutes before being reminded in unambiguous terms that 'being on the oars' should not be regarded as an opportunity to have a snooze, a fag, a cup of coffee or to indulge in birdwatching.

On South Uist there is much more to going fishing than catching fish.

TALES FROM THE ANGLER'S RETREAT

The Great Escapes

I have caught a lot of good brown trout on South Uist and Benbecula, including several over three pounds. But the fish I remember most clearly are the big ones that got away. Note the use of the words 'got away', not 'I lost'. I admit to having lost fish, lots of them; but the ones which got away did so by their own efforts rather than my incompetence. The three most memorable all escaped in the same way but each took the fly diifferently.

The first was during the best afternoon of fishing I have ever had, an afternoon of wading on the top part of East Bee. Before I left The Angler's Retreat that day James Paterson had given me one of his own tied flies, a size eight hook with a Green French Partridge head hackle and tail and a piece of cork on the shank. I had been a bit dubious about using it but, after fishing with no success for half an hour or so, I put it on thinking that it might just work in what was a strong wind and rough water. Fished on the dropper it made a wake like the Queen Mary and yet again I learned the importance of being willing to learn from a better angler. I caught five fish in about two and a half hours. Three of them were over three pounds each. All five were caught on that fly. The one that got away 'took' it too.

It was a 'bumper', a fish which follows and literally bumps or knocks the fly but doesn't take it. Half way through a retrieve I felt a bump on the fly. I did as I remembered having been told to do to by Billy on one of my early trips to South Uist: I kept retrieving at the same speed. Another bump, more retrieving, then a third bump. By this time the bob fly was so close to me that my rod was almost vertical and I was having to pull the leader across in front of me to keep the fly on the water. There was a fourth bump followed immediately by a hard take and the fish, a beautiful brown trout of at least three pounds, jumping straight up, full length out of the water, falling over and getting away.

The second was one morning I was fishing with Tony Smith and Ian Kennedy for salmon and sea trout on Roag. It was a wild morning but the only time loch fishing for salmon and sea trout when I actually believed I might hook a fish each time I cast. We fished all the usual places, doing drifts along the west, east and north banks and the sea trout lie. Ian had two pulls but neither fish was hooked. Tony and I didn't touch a fish. After about three hours we decided to fish the burn mouth and, as I had just been on the oars, I was given first shot at it.

The burn mouth is known as the Hole because the burn, when in spate, pushes away the sandy bottom on entering the loch, leaving a deep hole with a sand bank just beyond it. The normal method of fishing it is to beach the boat, wade out on to the sand bank and cast from there across the hole towards the far bank. On my second or maybe third cast I saw my point fly hit the water a few inches from the bank and started my retrieve. Almost immediately I felt not a pull or even a bump but what I can only describe as tic, tic, tic, as if the hook was being pulled through coarse sand or gravel. I knew this was impossible as the water was about nine or ten feet deep. It had to be a fish.

Sometimes when a fish takes you have time to think about what it and you are going to do. Not this time. Everything happened in the space of a few seconds. Tic, tic, tic, jump, a flash of silver, splash, gone. A sea trout which Ian reckoned was about five pounds.

The third fish was also on East Bee in a strong wind quite late on a bright, sunny afternoon. I had been wading out into the loch, fishing back in towards the shore with the sun behind me, retracing my steps, moving north a few yards and doing the same again; covering the water systematically, searching for fish. One of my casts was into a relatively calm little bay which was partly sheltered from the wind by rocks. I started my retrieve as soon as the point fly hit the water. The line tightened, then stopped. It felt as if I had caught a rock. I had waded along that shore a few days earlier and knew there was no rock. I waited for what seemed a very long time before the fish moved, very, very slowly along the shore to my right, towards the rocks. I had plenty of time to think about what it might do.

Because of the rocks it had to turn soon. It could come to my right, my left or straight towards me. My legs were wide apart, one foot on a rock below the water, bracing me against the wind. I moved them close together; no way was I going to have to admit to Billy that I lost a fish because I let it go through my legs! Whatever it did, I was sure it must start moving faster. But it didn't.

What it did was turn, heading out into the loch to my right, but no faster, still incredibly slowly. I had never known a fish move so slowly. I was retrieving line a few centimetres at a time, no more. I was sure it was a big fish. It is the big ones which move slowly. The tension was indescribable. It kept coming until it was alongside me, between me and the rocks. I turned to face it, carefully, trying not to spook it. It swam past me. Now I was letting line out centimetre by centimetre. I still could not believe how slowly it was moving. It turned again, into water on which the sun was reflected. And then, it jumped. From moving so slowly it suddenly and without warning shot out of the water like a missile from a submarine, straight up, a dark silhouette against the sun. And then of course it fell and was gone. I had been right about only one thing. It was a big fish.

The Jammy Bastard Trophy

By nature I tend not to like being the centre of attention. But in September 2006 I was going to be spending my 60th birthday at The Angler's Retreat. I couldn't let it pass without doing something to mark the occasion. So I sent Billy an email along the lines of 'Will be 60 on the 26th. Can't think of anything I would rather do than spend it on East Bee with you, Hamish and anyone else who will be there and wants to come. Can you book boats if this is OK?' His reply was typically Billy, generous but not without taking the chance to have a wee dig. 'Yes of course, but you're always jammy on that loch.' Me jammy? Never!

Another thing about me is that I don't like fishing competitions. They bring out the worst in me, which some unkind souls might say is mainly because I never win. What I did decide to do, but didn't tell anyone about in advance, was give a trophy to the person who caught the biggest fish. A magnificent cup all of five inches high made of the highest quality tin and plastic decorated tastefully with badly applied blue and imitation gold paint. For days before I set off for South Uist I tried to think what I should call it. 'The David Peutherer 60th Birthday Celebration East Bee Biggest Fish

Angling Competition Trophy 26th September 2006' didn't seem to be quite catchy enough. And anyway there wasn't nearly enough room to engrave it on the trophy, even if the tin had been thick enough to withstand the impact of the engraving tool, which it almost certainly wasn't.

On the day there were six of us in two boats: Billy, Hamish, Matthew, Chris, Mike and me (plus Fraser joining us for the morning). Now East Bee can be a superb loch to fish. It can also be dour, to say the least. I have had some of my best fishing days and caught some of my biggest fish on it. I have also had days when it would have been hard to convince someone fishing it for the first time that there were any fish there at all - and that they wouldn't have more fun spending the day reading the Gordon Brown Bumper Book of Stealth Tax Jokes, Volumes One to Six, while sitting

David's 60th birthday lunch by the Bee boat station. Sometimes photos fail to convey the full jollity of such occasions.

beside the loch being eaten alive by midges. My birthday was more dour than superb. I caught nothing, again. In fact the highlight for me, apart from the excellence of the company, was having lunch beside the loch, complete with Billy's famous kelly kettle.

I was expecting a normal dinner in the evening. After so many years of being the recipient of Marion and Billy's friendship and hospitality I should have known better. Marion had laid on a buffet especially for my birthday and, happily for me, had invited Hamish and Katy to come too. Champagne was drunk, stories were told and, embarrassingly but with much gratitude, presents were received.

In due course the presentation had to be made. Only one good fish had been caught, by Mike. A lovely two and a half pound trout, a fine example of the quality of fish which East Bee contains and a fish caught, it must be said, by a good fisherman and deserving of any trophy. In the process of racking my brain for a suitable name for it, I had only the day before remembered Billy's email. It brought to mind a term of endearment well known to Glaswegians. And so as I handed Mike the trophy, I said with all the generosity of heart and soul that I could muster for someone who had caught a bigger fish than me on my birthday 'It gives me great pleasure Mike to give you this, the appropriately named Jammy Bastard Trophy.'

I had typed the name on a bit of paper and glued it on to the base. The plastic looked slightly more substantial than the tin.

David's Favourite Uist Flies

BIBIO
Hook Kamasan, trout sub surface or heavy traditional, Size 12 or 10 **Thread** Black **Body** Black seal's fur, or substitute **Rib** Fine oval silver tinsel **Hackle** Black cock or hen
Fished on the point, the Bibio catches fish at any time of the season. I find it is most effective when tied nice and 'bushy' for summer/autumn and more sparsely dressed for early in the season.

CONNEMARA BLACK BUMBLE
Hook Size 12/10 **Thread** Black **Tail** Golden pheasant topping **Body** Black seal's fur **Body Hackle** Black cock or hen **Rib** Fine oval silver **Head Hackle** Partridge dyed blue, or jay
One of a number of 'bushy' flies which work well on the bob, or top dropper if using three flies. Others I use include the Claret Bumble and Kate McLaren and very easy-to-tie hackle flies with just black, claret or brown/red brown hackles, with or without silver or gold tinsel or wire. If the fish are hungry they will take any of them. The winged version of the Connemara Black works well on the point.

Mike Roberts

Arbroath

A Day on Roag

To take salmon and sea trout on the fly from a drifting boat has always been something special to me, but not something achieved very often by my fishing pal Peter Morrison and me on our annual visits to North Uist. Our success there has been largely confined to sea pools. But South Uist has a reputation for sea trout - and for producing the goods from a drifting boat. So in 2007, along with my regular fishing partner Dave Nicol, we decided to bite the bullet and book an August week at The Angler's Retreat.

The first morning, having devoured one of Marion's hearty breakfasts and one of Billy's detailed briefings, we drove through storm-swept terrain to Roag, one of the island's top salmon and sea trout lochs. After overnight rain, the loch was at a good level and carrying a peaty tinge. As soon as we got in the boat, Dave saw a sea trout splash as it entered the loch from the Howmore river, straight off the tide. Hopes rose as high as the wind!

We made several drifts along the west shore, all the time seeing fresh sea trout showing and seemingly running hard to the outlet burn from Fada, another of the premier league lochs. But we failed to connect with any of them. After lunch we fished the rest of the loch. Grilse showed all along the south bank but I was unable to control the boat in the ever-increasing wind. We decided to try from the bank and made to beach the boat.

Pete got out first and went headlong into the water. Although it was only inches deep, he got a thorough soaking. He struggled to get to his feet as the boat was still drifting, with him clinging to the side. Once ashore I thought this would bring a premature end to the day. However Pete insisted that Dave and I carry on fishing so

Mike & one from Roag that didn't get away.

114

Dave set to work casting in the burn mouth.

He was using a favourite blue muddler pattern, of which he had tied several prior to the holiday. Both Pete and I had cadged these muddlers from him over the previous few days and had some success with them. Now I asked Dave for another as, strangely, I couldn't find any in my fly box or on the front of my trusty fishing jumper, which is always adorned with flies. Dave said that he had just tied the last one to his cast - and that I should have taken more care with the ones he had given me!

Meanwhile a sodden, shivering Pete maintained a brave face. I suggested to Dave that we call it a day, but he insisted on one more cast. The next moment Pete sprang to his feet in excitement as Dave's rod bent into a fish. I ran over to Dave who insisted that it was only small, maybe about 2lbs. We saw nothing of the fish for five minutes as it fought deep and hard. At last Dave drew a beautiful fresh 6lb grilse to the surface and Pete made ready with the net. But all did not end well. Dave lowered the rod expecting Pete to raise the net. Pete misread the situation and withdrew the net thinking the fish was not ready. The hook hold gave and the fish was away!

We walked back to the car in silence, thinking what a difference that salmon on the bank would have made to the end of our day. We tackled down and took off our wet garments. I was unable to take off my jacket as it seemed stuck to the back of my jumper. Dave gave me a hand and then burst into laughter as he removed a hook from the back of my fishing jersey.

The mystery of the missing muddlers had been solved. I had obviously had a dram too many the night before and put my jumper on the wrong way round. It was now adorned with claret bumbles on the front and muddlers on the back.

Mike's Favourite Uist Fly

CLARET BUMBLE

Hook 8 or 10 Drennan Wet Fly Supreme **Tail** GP crest topped with Pearl Crystal Hair **Body** Claret seal fur **Rib** Gold or silver wire or tinsel **Body Hackles** Black and Claret cock wound together palmer style **Throat Hackles** Claret hen with dyed blue guinea fowl at the front.

You cannot go wrong for browns and seatrout with a claret bumble on the dropper. The bigger the wave, the larger and bushier the fly.

Bruce Sandison

Sutherland

Dreams come True in Uists and Benbecula

Arriving for the first time to fish North Uist, Benbecula and South Uist is like an angling dream come true. Driving west from Lochmaddy, you are confronted by a seemingly unending vista of lochs, some of which, like Loch Scadavay, are scattered with islands and tangled promontories, each of which are festooned with their own small lochs. Scadavay extends to the south of the A867 Lochmaddy to Clachan road and even this smaller southern section can provide several days sport.

The famous, lime-rich machair lochs that line the west coast are generally easily accessible from the main roads, but reaching many of the more remote east coast lochs requires a fair degree of fitness; as well as determination and the ability to use a compass and map. Also, be prepared for sudden, less than pleasant changes in the weather. In these parts a sunny day can turn into a nightmare quicker than you can mutter Grouse & Claret.

My wife, Ann, and I have fished in this wonderland for many years and never tire of going back for more. Each time we do, we discover new delights and new waters to explore. Many visitors make straight for the well-known lochs, such as East Loch Bee, Grogarry, Stilligarry, Bornish and West Loch Ollay on South Uist, justly famed for the quality of their wild brown trout. But, over the years, we have tramped ever further into the wilderness in search of the utter peace – and some really outstanding fishing – that only these places can provide.

South Uist is graced by three fine mountains, north to south, Hecla (606m), Ben Corodale (527m) and, the highest, graceful Beinn Mhor (620m). They dominate the eastern horizon and guard the approaches to three of the most remote lochs on the island, Spotal, Corodale and little loch Hellisdale. Find them on OS Map 22, Benbecula, Scale 1:50,000 at, respectively, grid references 834367, 831331, and 828310.

Hellisdale is best approached from the far end of the minor road at Arinambane (Gd ref: 792285) via Bealach Crosgard and Glen Liadale and it is reputed to hold some good trout. Head off for Corodale from the A865 at Grid ref: 768341. Aim for the bealach between Hecla and Ben Corodale then descend down Glen Usinish to reach the loch. As you do so, think of the fugitive Bonnie Prince Charlie; he tramped this way in 1746 when he hid from his pursuers and held 'court' in a cliff-top cave nearby.

My favourite, however, is Spotal, one of the loveliest lochs that I have ever fished. The last time I visited, I did so as part of an adventure hike from Loch Sgiopoirt (Gd ref: 829385) at the end of the B890. I tramped out past Loch Bein (Gd ref: 843373) to gain the north edge of the Ben Hecla horseshoe, then followed the ridge round over Beinn na h-Aire and Ben Scalavat to reach the summit of Hecla. I descend via Coir Rudale by tiny Loch a'Choire to fish Spotal.

Not so many years ago, sea-trout used to run to the loch from Loch Sgiopoirt and Caolas Mór, however, the advent of fish farming has brought an end to that. But Spotal still retains its magical grace and the brown trout, although not large, are big enough for me. As I turned to leave the loch, I noticed an otter watching me curiously from the far shore, and, overhead, the Hecla golden eagles marked my progress home across the moor.

Useless on South Uist

Being a Scot means that at an early age you are invariably introduced to the joys of rugby, golf and trout fishing. Well, to be precise, boys are, rather than girls, although my wife, Ann, has played golf and is also an angler. But as a boy, I was never particularly joyful with the rugby bit; lying under a muddy heap of vandals on a freezing Saturday morning did not seem to me to be the best way to spend precious school-free weekends.

Golf appealed for a while until my father, pushed beyond endurance, roared: 'Get out of my sight until you can watch where your damn ball goes!' This was understandable. Not only did it cost him a half a dozen balls to get me round, but it also took five hours and endless embarrassments with other players. I used to 'tack' up the course like a yacht in distress and only rarely on the fairway that I was meant to be playing.

That left trout fishing and none of my family fished. This seemed to be reason enough for becoming involved. At least I would be left to my own devices. No more twisted ankles and demonic sports masters. Goodbye to dissident fairways and scrabbling under gorse bushes searching for seriously slashed grey orbs of gutta-percha.

Fishing promised freedom, and even the worst duffer in the world has a chance of catching fish. In spite of what angling gurus might preach, believe me, if a fish is there, spots your fly and wants it, you will catch it. I have seen, all too often, so-called 'experts' ending the day red-faced and

East Loch Bee, looking southwest from near the boat station.

fishless whilst the duffer comes home with at least something for breakfast if not one for the glass case.

I persisted in this belief for years until the day I came eyeball to eyeball with the trout loch from hell: East Loch Bee on the Island of South Uist. I have thrashed bloody Bee to foam more times than I care to remember but have yet to take a decent fish from its shallow, brackish waters. Yes, I have caught trout, but fish so small that I hardly noticed them even although I was looking all the time.

A causeway divides the two sections of Loch Bee, east and west, and the whole system almost cuts the north end of South Uist in half, stopped from doing so only by floodgates at the east, Loch Sgiopoirt, end. Some South

Uist anglers claim that West Loch Bee is the more exciting fishery. It may well be but I can't really comment: the last time I fished West Bee if I had caught two more trout I would have had a brace.

What is beyond doubt, however, is that East Loch Bee is a first-class trout loch. My son, Blair, was Secretary of the South Uist Angling Club for a number of years and never missed an opportunity of sending regular details of fish that he and his friends took there, including gripping action shots of said fish being caught.

I have seen fish of over 4lb taken from East Loch Bee and, in spite of repeated failure, I keep going back; in the sure and certain knowledge that the longer I remain fishless, then the sooner it is that I will break my duck; or, in this case swan, because the loch is home to more than 100 of these graceful creatures. But tempus fugits and if I'm not careful I could find myself under these wretched gorse bushes again, hunting for lost golf balls.

The Right Place at the Right Time

Confidence is the name of the game. Being certain that you are in the right place at the right time. A state of affairs I seldom achieve. Invariably, upon arrival at my chosen location, eyes glinting, fingers twitching, I am greeted by the dreaded words:

'You should have been here last week. Still, have a bash. You never know your luck.'

I do. From years of bitter experience. Hopelessly lashing the water without seeing so much as a snout. Having to cope with telephone calls from so-called friends who follow me to the same fishing venue: 'What a week we have had! Just after you left the conditions were perfect. Never seen so many fish. They were almost giving themselves up.'

Not to me they don't. After more years fishing than I care to remember I confess I have yet to find any place in the world where they 'give themselves up'. I try to pretend that were they to do so much of the joy of fishing would vanish, but in all honesty, wouldn't it be nice, just for once, to be in the right place at the right time?

As the years of my fishing life lengthen I have come to accept the fact that catching fish is largely a question of luck. That it has very little to do with fine technique or vast knowledge, and even less to do with choice of flies. As long as your flies are in the water, then your chance of hooking your fair share is as good as anyone's.

I have discovered that changing flies doesn't really help. Consequently, I tend to rely on a few patterns and generally fish with them all day, indeed, all season. My favourites are the Black Pennell, Soldier Palmer, Ke-He, Woodcock & Hare-lug, Greenwell's Glory and Silver Butcher. And the Charlie Maclean, a unique Hebridean pattern that has brought me many fine fish. A 4lb 8oz wild brown trout from Loch Heilen in Caithness. A 9lb salmon from East Loch Ollay on South Uist, and many more. Well, a few.

I discovered this superb fly whilst researching my book The Sporting Gentleman's Gentleman and it has stood by me ever since. Charlie Maclean, now fishing that great trout loch in the sky, was a ghillie for South Uist Estate; a charming, gentle man who had a wonderful way with words, and a wonderful way with fish. The fly was devised by one of his guests as a mark of affection for Charlie's ability and unfailing courtesy.

The late Iain Christie, a solicitor in Portree on the Island of Skye, devised the fly. I contacted Iain to confirm a story Charlie told me about catching trout to music, which I found hard to believe. Charlie was fishing with Iain at the time on Loch Stilligarry, one of the famous South Uist machair lochs.

Stilligarry is a very special place; shallow, weedy, full of fishy corners and delightful little bays and islands. The quality of Stilligarry trout is quite outstanding. They are perfectly shaped with deep bodies and neat, small heads and they fight furiously. Persuading them to rise is the only problem. Stilligarry can be a dour, unforgiving place.

On this day, however, Charlie said that fish rose and were caught every time the song O-ho-ro Mo Chaillinn, sung in Gaelic by Calum Kennedy, was playing on Iain's portable tape recorder, which they had with them in the boat. Iain Christie confirmed that every word of the unlikely tale was true.

When Charlie died Iain sent me a few copies of the fly he was using at the time, and had named in honour of Charlie, and a full account of the incident:

'I was fishing with Charlie, again on Loch Stilligarry, one bright June afternoon in the early 1970's, in a north east wind. The fish were not moving to the usual flies in any of the usual places and Charlie rowed me across to the west side of the loch to a small bay, fringed with reeds, about one hundred yards south of the north-west corner of the loch.

'I put on the prototype of this fly and within an hour had caught three good fish on it, one of 3lb 8oz, the second 2lb 8oz, and the third being just under 2lb, all caught in and around that small bay. Charlie was very gratified that I named the fly after him, and you may be sure that it was suitably christened at the time.

'Since then I have had considerable success with the fly on many other waters, including the Storr Lochs here in Skye, and it does seem to bring up the bigger fish, although of course, it is not infallible. I usually fish it as my bob fly. If it catches a fish or two for you, I am sure it will have Charlie's silent approbation!'

I always fish the Charlie Maclean on the bob, with great confidence. It is a beautiful fly; lovely to look at and much appreciated by our fine friends below the waves. I hope that it brings you as much success and pleasure as it has brought me.

Bruce's Favourite Uist Fly

CHARLIE MACLEAN

Tail A short tuft of orange-red fluorescent wool
Tag In front of the tail, a couple of turns of flat silver tinsel
Rear hackle A few turns of white cock hackle tied in to slope backwards **Ribbing** Oval silver tinsel closely wound so as to leave just enough space between the turns to provide room for the stalk of the body hackle **Body Hackle** Furnace cock hackle, folded double. **Front Hackle** Two or three turns of white cock hackle, again tied in to slope backwards.
The singing lessons you will have to arrange for yourself and best wishes when you reach for that first high F sharp. But get the glass case ready – after all, you never know your luck.

Tony Smith

Morayshire

In the Beginning – Before The Angler's Retreat

It was around 1988 and I was serving at RAF Leuchars in Fife. I had heard about the trout fishing in South Uist and Benbecula from colleagues who worked at the radar site on North Uist and were stationed at RAF Benbecula. I persuaded my boss, also a fly fisherman, that we should pay a liaison visit to RAF Benbecula to discuss F4 fighter tactics with the resident fighter controllers.

We duly arrived at the Officers' Mess and completed our liaison business in double quick time. At dinner that evening, we made enquiries regarding the trout fishing as we had 'fortuitously' brought some tackle along with us! We introduced ourselves to the Secretary of the South Uist Angling Club, a civilian who lived in the Mess and he suggested we contact Warrant Officer Billy Felton, who worked at the Range Head. We duly made contact by telephone and arranged to meet Billy at his place of work up on the hill the next day. We were warmly received and immediately impressed with Billy's knowledge of the local lochs, and willingness to help us out.

For the remainder of our short stay, Billy steered us to which lochs to fish and generously offered to take us out for an evening session on his favourite loch, East Bee. It was during this first encounter that Billy's enduringly generous nature to brothers of the angle became evident. We were in many respects complete strangers but he lent us his old Landrover to tow his old black boat so we could fish on lochs not provided with boats. I recall, in true Billy tradition of make do and mend, the Landrover exhaust pipe hanging on with a bit of wire and that it could be heard approaching for miles around. However, in those days there was much less traffic on the islands and no one seemed to mind. We enjoyed some good fishing, in particular on one day when we were accompanied by Billy's youngest son, Fraser, who was living at home and about to join the Army. He ghillied us around East Olavat and I recall he was an extremely well mannered lad, who had something special about his demeanour; he greatly impressed me and in my mind I predicted he would go far in his chosen career.

We fished Loch Bee one day with some success, mainly casting to rising fish – yes, believe or not, fish did rise in those days. That evening Billy arranged to meet us at the loch after he had finished work to show us the ropes and the hidden parts of the loch. Initially we fished the main loch and we were most intrigued to witness Billy's casting technique, which in those days consisted of much false casting and laying the line on the water in front and behind the boat before the final cast. A technique we privately named Billy's 'lashing the water'. He also used an automatic reel, which we thought was a novelty, particularly as it always seemed to be jamming.

After an hour or so, Billy decided to show us the way to Middle Loch and beyond. After walking the boat from the main loch to the power lines, I recall the loch was always a lot shallower in those days, Billy took the oars and we commenced fishing. Our abiding memory to this day was that Billy was so keen to get through Middle Loch to show us Shell and the Sluice that he rowed like a man possessed. There were fish rising along the weed beds all the way down the loch but, despite our best efforts, lengthening the line and casting like fury, Billy kept on pulling the oars and the rising fish were left untouched.

After this initial visit, like so many others who will read these stories, I fell in love with Benbecula and South Uist, the fishing, scenery, wildlife, and the shooting. But most important of all, I formed a lasting friendship with Billy and Marion that has en-dured some twenty years. I was not surprised that when Billy retired he converted the family home into a guest house. He was so passionate about his fishing: it just had to be a success. As is now widely known, The Angler's Retreat has been a tre-mendous haven for anglers and

Tony with 4lbs 4ozs of West Ollay gold.

bird watchers amongst many others, which is a result of hard work, excellent catering and honest value for money coupled with unequalled hospitality.

My First South Uist Goose

I had never shot a goose on South Uist until Billy kindly invited me over to stay with him and assist with the goose cull programme. We set off early in the morning before first light and set up the decoys. I recall it was somewhere on the Bornish Machair. Throughout the morning, skeins of geese could be seen flighting up and down the machair but nothing came within range of our decoys. We decided to pack up and return to The Angler's Retreat for a much-welcomed breakfast. On the way back to the car, Billy suggested I had a pop at a couple of rabbits for the pot. I changed my heavy goose load to number six shot and duly despatched a couple of young rabbits. Then as we skirted the top of a dune, I spotted a skein of geese coming our way and I shouted to Billy to get down. As the geese flew past, having no time to change my load, I stood up and shot at the lead goose.

To my amazement, the goose behind the lead bird fell stone dead from the air. Billy's spaniel made a nice retrieve and we celebrated my first South Uist goose. That was an unlucky goose and until this day, to avoid a good ribbing, I have never had the heart to tell Billy that I was aiming at the first bird but got the second because I had not given the first one enough lead.

Foxhole Diplomacy

On another occasion, Billy and I were shooting geese on the Range over decoys from foxholes I had dug the previous evening. We were 30 yards apart with the decoy pattern placed in front of us. The first skein of geese attracted by the decoys passed in front of me and I killed one with my first barrel; they then veered off and out of range of Billy's position. He remonstrated with me, saying I should let them come to the decoys so we could both get a shot. We shot a few more geese between us and then, just as we decided to call it a day, a skein approached but passed just out of range. However, unknown to Billy a singleton flew straight over my head, which I shot. Billy heard the shot, immediately stood up and shouted indignantly 'Tony, I told you to let them come within range.' At that precise moment, the goose I had shot hit the ground with a thump, almost at his feet. Billy gave a wry smile and no more was said.

Tony's Favourite Uist Flies

TONY'S LOCH BEE SPECIAL
Hook Size 8/10 **Thread** Red **Tail** Lureflash orange vision bright fluorescent wool **Body** Holographic gold tinsel with a black palmered hackle **Rib** Gold wire **Head Hackle** Hot orange (three turns)

GREEN FRENCH PARTRIDGE

(Tony's version) **Hook** Long shank 10/12 **Thread** Black **Tail** Three or four pheasant tail fibres **Body** Olive and green seal's fur mixed **Rib** Silver wire **Head Hackle** French

---

Steven Walker

Falkirk

Three Go Mad in Uist

After a reasonable affair with Orkney, Sutherland and Caithness, my friends and I decided to take a trip to the Western Isles of Uist to meet Billy and Marion Felton at The Angler's Retreat. Having read about these famous machair lochs, we needed to get in them ourselves. The decision was a wise one and five years on we still make the annual pilgrimage. I've never missed a year. Shame I couldn't say the same about the fish – I've missed hundreds of them.

Billy is a mine of information to us all and is always there to point you in the right direction. A couple of phone calls before we arrive and he makes sure everything is in order. Whether it's fuel for the engine, packed lunches, directions to the lochs, you name it and he does it. At first we were a little cautious around Billy as he can be a tough old get, but give him a bit of respect and you will get quality fishing tips and the same respect back two times over. Maybe it's the army life still installed in him that makes him a hardy bit of tin. You'd better be there for breakfast in perfect time, always shut the gate so the cows don't eat the plants and NEVER EVER forget to return the packed lunch boxes! I'm not sure what would happen if you forgot but would never want to risk it.

The excitement starts as you head for the garage/rod room in the morning. Everyone is there getting their equipment ready, full of high hopes and filling the engines up for the day. The dog usually follows you around (knew I shouldn't have given her those midget gems five years ago) and, whatever the weather, Billy can pretty much forecast your day. He has a canny knack of telling you how it will pan out before you even leave the cottage. This is a good thing if the fishing has a chance of being good, but at the end of the day you have always got to stay positive in the Uists. Even the worst weather can bring some benefit.

Any small tips I got from Billy are remembered and honed very precisely. These small hints may have sounded vague at the time, but I've analysed them over and over in my head and, by using a bit of savvy, they might lead to the fish of a lifetime – not just for me but for the people around me too. I still remember most of them down to a T: that little set of skerries on West Ollay or fishing off the little dun on Cille Bhanain, the good drifts to hold on Grogarry, or when or where to wade on the big fish waters if the going gets tough.

The guy in the chip shop down at Daliburgh once asked me where I was staying. I started to say Billy Felton's and hadn't even got the second name out my mouth before the owner shouted, 'with Billy THE FISH?' That says it all really. Billy doesn't need to catch that four pounder from Grogarry or the bigger ones from West Ollay. He doesn't need to go out on Altabrug to catch 30 tiddlers to save his week like us guys. He's been doing it all his life. He's caught all the fish he needs. Who knows, maybe one day I will move there and try and attempt something the same as he's done.

Irish Bob. We have met Bob twice now at The Angler's Retreat. The first time he was with his wife and the pair were like a comedy act. Bob would tell a story and his wife would repeat the last half of each sentence. That king salmon Bob took in Alaska or the story of how Bob hated the baby doll, she knew them all. I'm not sure how many times she'd heard those stories before, but I'm guessing it was a lot. Bob was actually visiting Uist for two months this year. Two months! As he told me, 'What else do I have to do at this time in my life?' Sometimes I wish I could fast forward to a time when it's possible for me to fish in Uist for two months. Bob is a mean fly tier too. If you ever buy the bushy Kate's or dabblers from that wee box in Billy's lounge, then they came from Bob's vice. I remember he pulled a fly box from his boot one day not

Steven with one of the bigger ones from West Ollay.

long ago and passed me some flies. The rows of beautifully tied flies in that box were a sight to behold and having some handed to me was a joy. I still have them and hope to take a fish on them before this book is finished.

The Retreat has led me to meet some characters. Good people and good craic. Mind you, I have also shared breakfast there with some strange ones. Like the two bird watchers from the North East who looked like something from the *League of Gentlemen* TV series. I even had some Irish gypsies trying to sell me a power washer one year. Totally legitimate, they assured me.

One year there was a mix up over the caravan. Billy lined us up with another one and saved the day. But we hadn't been in this other one for fifteen minutes when the caravan door burst open. In staggered South Uist's answer to Ollie Reed – or was it Dracula. His face looked like it had just been sucking blood from a victim. I'm not sure if it was dark rum or red wine that had dried onto his face, but it had managed to form a kind of moustache and a set of fangs at the side of his mouth. He gave us a rendition of some song I can't remember and proceeded to tell some crazy but rather funny stories. Then he vanished, never to be seen again. The location and names we will leave out for obvious reasons.

The lochs tell their own story and some are famous for more than just fish. One day on Altabrug we had beached the boat as the fishing was slightly heavy going and we fancied a bit of lunch. Just after we had eaten we saw two bodies approaching with bobbly hats and red faces. Remember Tom Weir from *Weir's Way*? Well he wasn't one of them. But close enough. 'Hello', I said, 'How's it going?' They smiled and laughed. 'Yes we are fine, we are from Belgium and came to see the dun.' I said 'You came all the way from Belgium just to see the dun?' 'Yes,' they said. 'Can we have our pictures taken with you fishermen?' Of course, we replied. All that way to have their picture taken with a couple of grizzly fisherman? To be honest I hadn't paid much attention to the Dun. I was too busy looking for fish to be admiring ancient stones. They were just another fish holding area for me. I suppose we all travel to the islands for different reasons. There is something magical about the place. Something that draws you back time and time again.

One day while trying to enjoy a wee 40 winks at the side of Bornish, we got captured by a young burly Heilan girl with a big red shiny face. She'd managed to get a Vauxhall Astra lodged in a machair cowfield. The funny thing was it had BBC Radio Gaelic stamped on the side. The girl looked like she could eat a wee bit so I offered her a strawberry tart to try and calm her down, but she was that upset she declined. So we helped her dislodge her car from the field. (I hope her boss isn't reading this book or she might get her jotters.)

One Monday morning we arrived at the church on Bornish to find both boats were full. Were we double booked or was it the wrong loch? We were sure Billy had written down Bornish Monday on a piece of paper but I had mislaid it somewhere. We cursed him a bit for getting it wrong, but Billy was somewhere on Bee with Irish Bob and his phone was off. So we tracked down Captain John Kennedy to try and fix the mess. He had a wee blether with us from the pickup truck he drives and managed to sort it out. Turned out we were actually on Grogarry that day. Cackling away at Billy's expense, we made our way to the loch and managed to extract one well over three pounds and one well over four pounds, plus several two pounders. One of the best days we ever had on the loch. Billy said it was our fault and that we got all wrong, while our crew blamed Billy. Four days later we found the piece of paper and it read Grogarry Monday, Bornish Wednesday. Billy had been right all along. Thinking back now, the gods must have been with us – if the Bornish boats hadn't been full that day we might never have got those fish. We would have happily fished away on Bornish without even knowing the Grogarry fish were lining up to impale themselves on our hooks.

One wild day on Loch West Ollay – when the morning hailstorm was so hard it hurt but by 2.00pm I was sunburnt – I had tried Blobs, Cats Whiskers and every other concoction in my box. At 4.00pm I went back to basics, a Butcher and a Zulu, and by 4.15pm I had caught a four and a half pounder. I've never hit the five pounder, yet, but it doesn't matter as that West Ollay fish was the best fish I've ever seen with my own two eyes. It will live with me for a long time – a fit cock fish whose tail, back and fins were pure buttery gold. I could never kill a fish like that. I managed to get a full camping kit and tent with my Hebrides Fish of the Month prize money and I also got a trophy to prove it. I was more than chuffed.

My friends have also had some very good fish from the lochs. Derek and Stew have had a good lot of two pounders and the odd three pounder between them and Dominic has probably had the largest fish but maybe fewer fish in total. Last year I ribbed him for months before we visited telling him how he was past it and that his trout catching days were a distant memory. I wish I had kept my mouth well and truly shut. Over two days he managed to extract some of the finest looking fish I ever saw – a cracking fish of around four pounds just off the island on Grogarry and an even bigger one from the small narrow channel just out from the noust. That bigger fish was as long as your arm and quite slender. If it had been fully fit and filled out I hate to think how big it could have been. That's not to mention the two pounders he's had or one about four pounds from a wee set of hill lochs Billy sent us to about five years ago.

Talking of Billy and hill lochs, never ever tell him you fancy a stretch of the legs or somewhere off the main roads to fish for the day. I sweated so much on one of those expeditions that I had to empty my waders of perspiration at the loch side. One loch was so rocky on the bottom I managed to gently slip and totally submerse my whole body. I went under for a few seconds. The funniest part must have been for Dominic forty yards downshore from me. Moments before he had shouted at me to ask what flies I had on. When he looked back up I had completely disappeared, 25 yards out from the shore. He panicked for a second, only to see the water

erupt as a human torpedo shot into the air. What a dunking I got. I ended up completely naked at the side of some hill loch trying to dry my clothes in the sun with a fly rod in my hand.

Marion Felton? The woman is a Living Legend! Myself and my friends always stay in the caravan

Dominic's 'slender' monster from Grogarry.

130

when we visit, which is usually self-catering. But we managed to get Billy to sweet talk Marion into making breakfast for us in the house. It's a cosy arrangement. We arrive at eight before the guests come down and Marion potters away on the large Aga hob while we read the weather and chat away. We perch high on the breakfast bar in the kitchen while Marion serves us bacon and eggs and the whole works. 'Boys, you're part of the family now, sitting on my breakfast bar with me making your breakfasts,' she would say. I think Marion likes having us in there for a chat as we would always give her the banter – and she takes as good as she gets. Must be the Essex girl in her. Always up for a giggle and never burns the toast. How we enjoy sitting there on those high stools looking out the window, while fattening ourselves for the day ahead and having all the laughs with Marion. One of the nicest down to earth folk you will ever meet.

Nothing is ever a hassle for Billy and Marion. We will sadly miss going to The Angler's Retreat when they retire.

Steven's Favourite Uist Flies

GOLDEN OLIVE BUMBLE
Hook 10 or 12 **Thread** Black
Body Frankie McPhillips Golden Bumble Olive Dubbing
Rib Fine gold wire **Palmered Hackle** Golden olive cock
Head Hackle Red game cock or picric hen
Tail Hot orange tippet (non-standard tying)

GREEN PETER MUDDLER
Hook 10 or 12 **Thread** Black
Body Frankie McPhillips Olive seal's fur **Rib** Fine gold wire
Palmered Hackle Red game cock **Wing** Hen pheasant
Head Dark brown or olive deer hair

Mike Warwick

Edinburgh

Playing Colonel Bogie

I first stayed at The Angler's Retreat with my father, Ralph, in 2006. That was my first trip to the Hebrides. I loved Benbecula and South Uist and greatly enjoyed the hospitality offered by Marion and Billy. I have returned there with Dad once or twice a year since, depending on how much time I can reasonably spend away fishing without my wife Sarah and our twins, Heather and Beth.

In the many hours Billy has generously spent fishing with us, he has taught us a great deal – about fishing, obviously, but also about boat handling, birdlife, other wildlife and the history of the Uists. To mention but a few things. I'm sure we have all learned much from him and Marion.

I sneaked in an extra weekend on my own at the beginning of October this year – I could make a case given that I was on the doorstep anyway (well, almost) doing some work in Portree on Skye. I caught some nice trout including a 2-plus pounder, bigger than I've previously managed in Uist. Billy also took me shooting with him and Raven one evening. It was great to see the pair of them in action and to learn something from Billy about a pursuit I knew nothing about. I had no idea ducks could move so fast. And they were very hard to spot in the dusk. Clearly, Billy is a major authority on wildfowling, particularly on South Uist.

Back at the beginning of my stays at The Angler's Retreat, something unfortunate happened. I didn't know Billy and Marion very well, as it was only the second night I had spent there. I was staying in one of the upstairs rooms and Dad was in the other. As it was quite warm, I'd had the window open in the evening to try to cool the room down a bit. When I went up to bed there were a lot of insects in my room so I shut the window and killed off what I could that I thought might bite me. To try to reduce the heat in the night I opened the window in the seating area outside the room at the top of the stairs. Bad mistake!

It rained in the night. Dad woke me up saying 'Is this flood anything to do with you?' It was horrendous. So much water had flowed down the window and onto the landing that the wastepaper basket which had caught a small proportion of it was two thirds full. The rest was in the TV, on the carpet and soaked through the floor.

There was nothing I could do to cover this up. A confession had to be made. I wasn't sure how Billy would react. I thought that, whatever happened, I would be likely to find the place solidly booked up in the future, at least as far as I was concerned. However, in the typically generous and straightforward manner that I learned from then is Billy's way, he was very understanding about the accident. He looked immediately towards the bright side – insurance payout for a new TV! I was grateful for that and felt it unlikely that I would have taken it quite so well, had I been him.

Mike (in white hat) fishes near the Sluice Gate on East Bee.

Billy said on our trip this year that he considers himself to be a retired serviceman, and proud of it, rather than a civilian. This will come as no surprise to those that know him and have fished with him – his organisational skills and ability to keep a boat ship-shape are a lesson in themselves. I have sometimes felt, as a more junior male guest, that Billy directs a bit of his Sergeant Major side towards me now and again. But very gently, of course. For example, let no young man on the oars ever doubt that he must do exactly what the Captain says. I remember one time on East Olavat, I was rowing the boat through the difficult narrows to the boat station, under Billy's direction. I was sitting on a cushion that was impeding my ability to

133

dip my hands low enough over my knees to clear the oars from the water. I tried repeatedly to pause the rowing for a fraction to remove the cushion but this was impossible – every time I tried Billy commanded 'Keep going'. In the end, I got Dad to move the cushion. Having said this, learning about handling a boat and ghillying from Billy has been great fun and immensely valuable.

As we can all attest to, Billy's straightforward observations and skills as a raconteur have always served to keep his guests amused and informed. These are a few Billy moments that have stuck in my mind:

I had a bad couple of days with one of the outboards refusing to start much of the time. I tried what I could including using the choke with variable success. On the second of these days Billy was nearby – in the other boat on Loch East Bee. I asked him later if he had any idea why I couldn't make the outboard work reliably and he said 'I saw you playing Colonel Bogie with the choke. The engine won't work if you play Colonel Bogie with the choke!'

Chris and Matthew will remember our amusement one evening when Billy was talking about the 'Rah-rahs in the Lochboisdale Hotel'. 'Rah, rah, rah' he was saying. And the classic thing about it was he was looking up the nose of a rah-rah at the time!

A day when we took the spinning rods down to the far end of Loch Bee. Dad and Billy were sitting on the bank while I had a few casts. On one rather heroic effort the lure pinged off at the most powerful point of the cast and arched away a very long distance. Billy stopped talking for a few seconds. Then I turned to walk back in and he realised the lure had snapped off. He said, 'For a moment there we were quite impressed.'

A rather dour day on Dun na Cille. The wind was quite strong and Billy was on the oars, talking about how everyone does an equal share, etc. We came round a point and into a significantly calmer area. I said 'Excellent, I'll do my ghillying here then'. Predictable response from Billy – 'Ralph, what sort of a son have you go here? Give him a few years with me in the army!'

Dad on the oars on Langavat, me and Billy fishing. I had one of those spells where a wee fankle is followed by another wee fankle and another, etc. Billy tends to say at these times 'I'm not involved at all. It's got f*** all to do with me.' While I was undoing a fankle, Dad was telling Billy when we started fishing together and how long ago that now was. Billy said 'So how did he get to the standard he is now then?' When I gave no response he said 'Michael's not going to rise to it, he's too busy doing his knitting or something.' Then added 'I'll tell you how to straighten out that line. Grow runner beans up it. And buy a new one to fish with.'

This year Billy showed us the caravan and told Dad he is on the list of people he would trust to stay there after he and Marion retire. This is obviously very generous of Marion and Billy and we may well do so. I said to Billy 'I imagine I'm not on the list unless I'm with Dad'. Predictably the answer was 'Yes, that's true, you're not.' And who can blame him for that after the flooding incident!

When I left after my last weekend Billy very generously gave me two geese to take home – one for me and one for Dad. He told me that one had been gutted and frozen, and the other was fresh and needed to be dealt with from scratch when it got to Edinburgh. I said that the fresh one would clearly be Dad's then. Billy said, 'It is my view that your father has failed with you. My sons wouldn't think that way'. I said, 'I think it but wouldn't do it'. Billy replied, 'None of my sons would even think that way'. He said he'd phone Dad to check which goose I gave him! We actually ate the two geese together – shared between me, Sarah, Dad, Mum and Dad's brother and his wife. They were great and appreciated by all. A very generous gift. And yes, I did do the prep myself!

Mike's Favourite Uist Flies

YELLOW FRENCH PARTRIDGE
A variant of the Green French Partridge (See Brian Concannon), with yellow instead of green seal's fur on the body.

SOLDIER PALMER MUDDLER
Hook Size 10, long shank **Thread** Red or brown
Tail Fluorescent red floss **Rib** Fine oval gold tinsel
Body Red seal's fur, or substitute **Hackle** Brown cock
Collar Hackle Soft-fibred brown cock

Ralph Warwick

Mid Lothian

The Master's Apprentices

I first met Billy in June 2004 when my wife Lilian and I were island hopping from Barra northwards and stayed at the Benbecula Hotel for a couple of days. I saw The Angler's Retreat sign as we were driving past one day and couldn't resist ringing the bell for a chat. Billy wasn't feeling well, otherwise I expect he would have been on a loch somewhere. Nevertheless, with typical kindness, he welcomed me in. Half an hour later I left with his brochure, John Kennedy's book and a firm intention to return.

I have visited twice per year since 2006, sometimes alone and sometimes with my son, Michael. We have both greatly appreciated the warm hospitality offered, Marion's excellent breakfasts and ample dinners and, of course, Billy's guidance and tuition in the gentle art of catching South Uist brownies.

Our most recent visit was two weeks ago as I write this, in the third week of August 2008. The following are the highlights of four whole days which the Master spent fishing with us. Had we not been blown off on our last day, he would have spent a fifth. Of course on that day he recommended a choice of bank fishing that could still be attempted in a strong south easterly wind.

Our first outing was on East Bee with two boats, Billy and a delightful Welshman called Arwel in one and Michael and I in the other. It has to be said that the fishing was slow, but Michael caught a hard fighting one pounder and Arwel was delighted to bag five, the biggest being about 1½lb and his best trout ever. East Bee was lovely as always and, of course, there were numerous swans putting up with our intrusion. We also saw two big flights of widgeon and the occasional raven on our run down to the bottom cut which, understandably, is Billy's favourite place on the loch. There, at this farthest point from the road, had we been alone, a nightmare scenario would have developed. Our engine ran out of fuel as we arrived and, inexplicably, the fuel cap had become so tight that none of us could budge it. Out came Billy's trusty tool kit. Everybody's heart but Billy's sank when we saw there was no wrench. We weren't optimistic when Billy used a pair of pliers as a hammer to give some sharp blows to the knurled rim of the cap. However, we should have had faith because he had the cap off in three minutes!

Two days later we were on Loch Dun na Cille in reasonable conditions. The trout were sulking but we had an excellent view of an osprey, the first that Billy had seen on the islands. A beautiful place, although the fishing was dour. Happily, Billy showed us a brackish pool on the way home where I caught a lovely 1½ lb brownie that saved the day and was the best fish of our holiday.

Next day we were on the long, narrow, charming Loch Langavat which has its own special beauty and, blimey, within a few minutes we had a fantastic close view of a sea eagle which lasted for several minutes. We saw it again in bright sunlight directly above the boat at one point later in the day. We also collected rowan berries from trees overhanging the loch with which Marion made a lovely, flavoursome, deep coloured jelly. She kindly gave us each a jar. The fishing however, was slow again – Billy said that our bag of seven three-quarter pounders would have been twenty or thirty-seven on an average day on that 'free rising' water. We'll be going back, hoping for an average day, I'm sure.

Our fourth outing was on Loch Hallan. Again, the conditions were reasonable but the bird watching better than the fishing. By the time we gave up on floating lines we had seen a peregrine speeding by. Polyleaders and intermediates didn't fare much better and Billy had a go with the dapping rod. After three-quarters of an hour intense concentration Billy was distracted by a hen harrier diving on a rabbit that ran off terrified. A trout saw its chance and rose to Billy's fly. 'Bugger!' said Billy. 'If it wasn't for that bloody harrier I'd have had that trout.' Whereupon Michael said, 'The harrier's probably saying 'Bugger, if it wasn't for Billy I'd have had that rabbit.'

Michael then tried a dry fly and, with some useful coaching from Billy, caught a one and a quarter pounder - his best fish of the holiday. We scored a hat-trick for raptors when a kestrel obligingly appeared and hovered for us.

So, those were our four days. Rather disappointing fishing, but much compensation in the varied, wild and lovely places we visited and the wonderful wildlife we encountered. And, of course, the continuation of our fishing apprenticeship with Billy, who kept us entertained throughout with his wit, wisdom and fund of stories.

Ralph's Favourite Uist Flies

SOLDIER PALMER
Hook Sizes 12, 10, 8 **Thread** Brown **Tail** Red wool
Body Red wool **Hackle** Brown or red/brown cock hackle
with one or two turns of longer hackle behind the head
Rib Fine gold oval tinsel

GOAT'S TOE
Hook 12, 10, 8 **Thread** Black **Tail** Red wool **Body** Bronze
peacock herl **Rib** Red floss or silver oval tinsel as variant
Hackle Blue peacock neck feather tied behind the head

Richard Woodall & David New
Cumbria

Wildlife Wonderland

RICHARD 'BAR' WOODALL: I first visited North Uist many years ago with my wife and friends. We stayed at the Lochmaddy Hotel and fished their lovely lochs. We were so impressed by the remote beauty of the islands that I vowed to return. Due to business and other family holiday arrangements it was not until 2005 that I was able to do so, with my friend David New. We stayed at The Angler's Retreat with Billy and Marion Felton. Unknowingly we were so fortunate in our choice of accommodation because Marion and Billy were truly wonderful hosts. Another huge slice of luck was when Billy very kindly offered to be our ghillie for the week.

In the house Marion reigned supreme and was charming company – a great cook, her meals are legendary. I recall mentioning that I enjoyed a good rabbit pie, having been reminded of it by seeing so many wild rabbits on the island. Sure enough half way through our stay rabbit pie was served! Marion is one of those wonderful people who get an enormous amount of pleasure out of producing her guests' favourite dishes. Her food was great.

Meal times are a most important social event at The Angler's Retreat because Billy and Marion invite all their guests to join them at the dining table. It is so enjoyable to be in the company of such convivial people and to swap yarns of the day's events. I must say how very much both David and I appreciated the company during our holidays there and that it was great to find we were all on the same wavelength!

One of the many attractions of the Uists is that they are totally unspoilt and get the full force of the Atlantic weather. They also welcome a very healthy run of salmon and sea trout which were the quarry that David and I were interested in.

From a purely fishing point of view South Uist is an angler's paradise with beautiful lochs which it is a privilege to fish. We had some most enjoyable fishing on Mill Loch whilst Roag proved to be our best for salmon. On our first visit there I managed to connect with and land a nice fresh fish of 6 lbs and, as we all know, there is nothing like a bit of success to both lift the spirit and keep one on one's toes. One of the great advantages of fishing on South Uist is that many of the lochs are readily accessible. For someone like me who, to use modern terminology, is well past his 'sell by date' this is a godsend.

On our second visit in 2006 we again commenced our week's 'work' on Mill Loch and, whilst not seeing any migratory fish, enjoyed some good sport with trout in the half to one pound size. Loch Roag was our port of call the next day and David duly obliged by catching a nice fish of 6 lbs. We then fished Loch Fada where, although it was very bright, there was a good breeze. (Sometimes when the wind is blowing in from the Atlantic there is far too much 'breeze'!) David produced another nice fish and it was most encouraging to see many more salmon there, although we only managed to extract one. We also fished the lovely Loch East Bee which, like most Hebridean lochs, was fairly shallow and had many really attractive drifts.

Time spent fishing in the company of Billy is one of the most enjoyable experiences one can have. Not only is he a first class fisherman, he has also become an authority on the wildlife, especially the birdlife. During our two visits there we witnessed quite a lot of the wildlife. For example there were literally thousands of wild geese flying over us much of the time and Billy told us something that I never knew – the fact that wild geese actually sleep while they are on the wing.

On one occasion when returning from fishing one day an otter quite nonchalantly walked across the road in front of the car. We stopped and got out to get a better look at it but it had simply vanished, until we saw that about twenty yards away there was a small pool of water not much bigger than a puddle. Sure enough, following the slightest movement on the surface the otter poked his head out of the 'puddle', as if to see what we were up to.

Billy also told a wonderful story about the corncrakes which still survive on the islands. One evening he answered the telephone and was asked, 'If my wife and I come to Uist could you tell us where to see and hear a corncrake?' Billy said he could. At that time a corncrake was actually 'living' in Billy and Marion's garden. The visitors duly arrived to stay for a week but left after two nights, muttering words to the effect: 'That damned corncrake has squawked all night long and neither of us has had a wink of sleep since we arrived.'

Not even Marion and Billy can please everyone.

A Memorable Day on South Uist

DAVID NEW: In September 2005 Bar Woodall and I spent a day fishing for salmon and sea trout with Billy on Loch Fada. In the morning there was a good breeze with glimpses of sunshine, but not even one glimpse of a fish. We lunched in the fishermens' hut on the east bank before setting out to fish again in the afternoon. We covered all the usual lies along the east and west shores and in the bays, but with the same result – no fish.

Towards teatime Billy suggested that, as the standard fly patterns which we had been using all day had failed, we should try something else. Anything we wished, was how he put it. At that time there was a good salmon wave on the water. I put a size ten muddler with a red tag on the dropper and a size ten double traditionally-tied Parmachene Belle on the point.

At four o'clock we were drifting along the north end of the east shore, casting into the shallows, when a swirl on the water was followed by a heavy pull then an explosion as a good fish took the Parmachene Belle. At first it ran close in and parallel to the shore but then, as if it had got its bearings and decided what to do, swam at top speed towards deep water.

Bar retrieved his line to make sure it didn't get tangled with mine, and grabbed his camera. Billy too knew exactly what to do; he rowed away from the shore, following the fish into the deep water.

Having arrived at the place which the fish had chosen as its

David New and Bar Woodall.

141

hiding place I was amazed to discover that, rather than having on the end of my line a fish which was running and pulling powerfully, I had a heavy, stationary weight. Billy said the fish had run into a bed of weed, which can best be described as freshwater kelp. I applied pressure and slowly pulled a mass of closely gathered weed towards the surface where it lay in the water like a raft, a raft which had my line going in at one end and, sticking out the other end, the tail of a salmon, gently quivering as if indicating that it believed it was safely hidden from sight.

What with the weight of the weed and the salmon, the hook was obviously under extreme pressure. A decision was made: an attempt had to be made to net the fish, weed and all. Billy went for it, gathering weed and fish into the net then depositing in the bottom of the boat a huge pile of 'kelp' with my fish somewhere inside it. As if the fish had suddenly realised its cover had been blown, it burst into life before Billy grasped it and despatched it with a swift blow.

I will always remember the sight of the salmon's flank gleaming in the sunshine alongside Billy's beaming smile as he held high our prize of a 7.5lb cock salmon. The Parmachene Belle had saved the day again. The salmon certainly knew what he was after, and almost found the perfect hiding place. But Billy knew better!

David's Favourite Uist Fly

PARMACHENE BELLE

Hook Size ten, double **Body** Yellow floss silk or wool
Rib Flat gold tinsel **Wings** White duck or swan with a stripe
of red ibis feather on each side; the ibis should be about
half the width of the duck or swan **Hackle** Dyed scarlet
cock mixed with white cock **Tail** Red and white duck
*The Parmachene Belle has worked for me in places such as South Uist,
South Harris and Western Ireland. My first one was given to me many
moons ago by my Grandfather when I was a child and he gave me flies to
put in a Hardy fly box which had been given to me by my parents one
Christmas. The Parmachene Belle is one of those gaudy patterns which
quite possibly never worked for my Grandfather in the Lake District where
he fished. The best conditions for it seem to be a loch with a good
breeze combined with bright sunshine.*

PAST TALES

From the 1951 edition of The Fishing Inns of Scotland.

Physicians A-Fishing

Four doctor pals from Newcastle fished the lochs of South Uist each year during the late nineteenth and early twentieth centuries. In 1906 they published a poem about their exploits. It could easily have been written by regulars from The Angler's Retreat one hundred years later. Here's an extract from what they wrote:

O reach the Western Hebrides
The angler braves the stormy seas
But if he'd go where trout are fewest
You bet it won't be to South Uist!
There sport is good as heart could wish,
And one can hardly fish for fish.
For this, with souls that would not flinch,
And stomachs firm, we've crossed the Minch.
With what success will soon appear.
But let us first explain that we're
Four cronies from the banks of Tyne,
All decent chaps as e'er cast line,
Or told a pack of fishey lies,
Or cussed the trout that wouldn't rise.

And me, Oh Muse! To sing the praise,
Of Crogovat, of many bays,
And shallows, where the brown trout bask
As close as herrings in a cask;
With rock and weed, for hold and feed –
An angler's paradise indeed!
Short time to gaze; our tackle ready,
'Into the boat! Allright! Now, Steady!'
Then off we glide. The faithful Neil –
That prince of ghillies – guides the keel.

144

The trout, at first, decline to rise,
And scorn our most alluring flies.
The loch is smooth; the air is calm.
The sky is bright; we mutter 'D—n!'
This for an hour. Wind comes at last;
The blazing sun is overcast;
The waters ripple. 'There's a rise,'
'Hooked.' 'There's another; what a size!'
He's hooked as well. Neil, nothing loth,
With gentle chuckle, soon nets both.

The loch, awhile ago so quiet,
Boils like a pot with piscine riot,
The trout before were dull;
next minute
They take as if the deuce were in it!
A fish or two at ev'ry cast
Is sport too good, you'll say to last:
But last it *did*, beyond a doubt,
Till we gave over, quite worn out.

Thus day by day runs past in sport,
And merry tales make evening short,
Till, all too soon, our time flown by,
We leave Lochboisdale with a sigh.

Historical Writings

Newspapers started reporting on the sport fishing of South Uist and Benbecula from the mid eighteenth century. A handful of anglers have also published accounts of fishing there over the past century or so.

Aberdeen Journal 19th November 1845

In an article entitled Improvements in the Long Island, the paper reported on work undertaken in Colonel Gordon's estates on Barra, Uist and Benbecula. These included building a road from North to South and digging a large canal with floodgates to drain Loch Bee.

The Scotsman 13th May 1880

'Benbecula is an uninteresting island, with no considerable hills to diversify the dreary monotony of its surface. There is no good accommodation for tourists, and the fishing is not open to the public.'

The Times 16th August 1883

The paper prints a long guide to angling in South Uist, which it describes as 'the finest fishing in Scotland'. It recommends staying at the Lochboisdale Hotel and fishing lochs A Bharp, Kildonan and Creanabreck, with excellent bank fishing everywhere. It claims it is easy to hook three and four pound sea trout in Strome Dearg, but just as easy to lose them in the weed; apparently Lady Cathcart is about to start building a floodgate there. The Howmore River, though only half a mile long, offers 'most excellent though privileged sport – the best in Scotland'.

Aberdeen Weekly Journal 30th August 1893

'Benbecula Moors and Lochs. Sir William Smythe, lessee of the Benbecula shootings, has had splendid sport this week on the moors and lochs of that island. As an instance, on one day he bagged 25 wild ducks, while on another day he landed 23 freshwater eels, averaging about two feet in length each. Another gentleman landed 20 trout at Loch Bee weighing 27lbs.'

Angling at Lochboisdale, R.A. Chrystal

This writer uses the hotel's fishing log to create a detailed account of fishing there during the early twentieth century. Average trout sizes do not appear to be large, eg: '1922: Undistinguished brown trout fishing during May, June and July, but only in May and June is the half pound average exceeded, the June catches being nearer three to the pound. A number of trout over 1lb from Lower Bornish and one actually 2lbs.' Earlier Chrystal reported that 'The outstanding event of 1907 was that a dam was erected, closing Strome Dearg and cutting it off from Hallan.' Given that the Times first reported plans for this dam in 1883 (see above), it took a mere 24 years to arrive. But it proved very valuable in stopping crofting land from being submerged by spring tides.

Fifty Years Angling, Joseph Adams 1938

In this grand account of fishing across England, Scotland, the Hebrides, Ireland, Holland, Switzerland and Canada, Joseph Adams includes a chapter on fishing Loch Bee. He describes West Bee as more fished than East Bee, with boats kept only on one side and dragged through a passage beneath the road when necessary. The first fish he hooks, having no depth to dive, makes straight off. Thinking it to be at least 3lbs in weight, he is surprised to find it but a pound. 'But what a beautiful fish; its sides were golden, its spots the most brilliant red, shapely as a well-bred fish ought to be, with small head and broad shoulders.' He goes on to describe the large flocks of whooper swans, which superstitious islanders leave well alone.

Going Fishing, Negley Farson 1942

'At South Uist we went ashore, saw the verandah of the hotel literally paved with sea trout – and we were told that the average for that year had been 2.5lbs! This was the famous Loch Boisdale, perhaps the finest sea trout fishing in the British Isles. But we were told that we could not fish there: all the beats were taken up. 'What is more,' said the proprietor, with almost sadistic pleasure, 'you'll no be able to fish here next season. I'm all booked up.' But strangely enough, it is one place that I have no wish to go back to.

The fishing seemed almost a business there. It was too well organised. Still, if you want to be sure of catching masses of fine sea trout, that's the place.'

The Western Isles, Alasdair Alpin MacGregor 1949

'The wholesale introduction into the Islands of the motor-car in recent years has made poaching much easier than it used to be. It enables the owner to reach, in ease and comfort, many a distant loch noted for its brown trout, or a remote spot where a bit of shooting can be done on the sly. He will often pack into his car such as of his friends as know precisely where the best sport may be poached. Much of this poaching is done at night, of course, when conditions are favourable. The whisky-bottle is usually an indispensable accessory on such unlawful occasions.'

Dean Monro's 1549 Description of the Western Isles of Scotland

Going back some time, this Sixteenth Century observer wrote of a fish trap on Loch Bee: 'In this isle there are infinite number of freshwater lochs; but there is one main loch called Lochebi, three miles long, and an arm of the sea has worn the earth . . . and in that narrow entry that the sea has gotten to the loch, the countrymen have built up a thick dyke of rough stones, and penny stones cast long nearest (set lengthways), notwithstanding the flowing streams of the sea enter through the said dyke of stones in the said freshwater loch, and so there is continually getting stuck among the rough-stones of the dyke aforesaid, fluke, pollack, skate and herring.'

Frederick Rea

'Reminiscences of a Hebridean Schoolmaster, 1890-1913' is a fascinating glimpse into life on South Uist during the late Victorian period. Its author F.G. Rea learnt to fish while on the island and, like many before and since, became mildly obsessed with tapping the riches of the fishing there.

Cross-country trout

One Saturday afternoon I happened to be at Lochboisdale pier when I met Duncan, the hotel keeper's son, with his fishing rod. I accompanied him to a neighbouring loch and watched him casting. Nothing happened for a time; then there was a swirl in the water; he struck and hooked a fish which had taken his tail-fly. After a few rushes and runs the fish was netted and landed – a nice five-pound fish. Duncan killed it with a blow on the head. He was then about to remove the hook from where it had caught in the fish's lip, when we saw a broken cast of three flies was hanging from the side of its mouth. 'Greedy beggar!' was Duncan's comment.

Returning to the hotel we found that parties of anglers had returned and were laying out their respective 'catches' on the grass in front of the hotel, and were comparing them. We told them of the fish we had caught and of the broken cast. Much surprise was shown and one of them said, 'One fish broke me and got away with the cast. But it could not be the same fish for it was on Loch K – – –, and that is quite eight miles away?' Then one of the other anglers asked whether he remembered what flies he had on the cast at the time. Quite readily he gave them: march brown, teal and green, and zulu. Duncan went indoors, then returned with the cast. This on examination convinces us that it came from the identical fish that had been hooked earlier in the day. It must have travelled for miles through a chain of lochs only to be killed eventually near the sea in the evening of the same day.

Cross the stream on their backs

As the weather was fine Craig proposed to me that we should walk home along the 'machair', and the proposal met with my immediate acceptance for the summer beauty of the beflowered shore-lands was then at its fullest. . . . Some two miles had been covered when Craig, who was a short way ahead, stopped and stood looking downwards, at the same time giving to us a low call 'Come here'. Quietly hastening to his side we found that he was looking intently into a stream that was running towards the sea, and directly across our path. The stream was about six or seven feet in width and running in a clean-cut channel across the 'machair'. At first I did not see what he was gazing at; then I became aware that hundreds and hundreds of trout were rushing inland up the stream; they were so closely packed that the water seemed scarcely sufficient to contain them. We all stood silently watching them as they sped past us at our feet: all sizes of fish from a foot to three or four feet in length were hurrying madly upstream: so thick were they in the water that even the big fish seemed to find difficulty getting past their smaller brethren and, by sheer strength and their weight, they forced their way through the packs of speeding fish.

We stood watching them for nearly an hour, and still then the stream was packed as full of them – there must have been thousands of them – I remember remarking to my companions: 'We could almost walk across the stream on their backs!' Craig, at last, gave a deep breath and said in a voice full of feeling: 'Well, boy and man I have fished the eastern rivers of Scotland, from the Ythan to the Tweed, but I have never seen such a sight as this before.' Alasdair told us that this stream was an effluent of the Howmore River and these waters were strictly watched and preserved for the sport of the proprietor and his friends. He had often seen the trout ascending the stream, but he had never seen them in such numbers before. Here we had to part with our friend; so, giving one last look at the fish we so much coveted, we each stepped back a few paces, took a run forward and leapt the stream. Not trusting ourselves to look into it again we waved to Alasdair and resumed our way homeward.

The Monster Trout

On inquiring from our friend of the inn, we were assured that the report about the monster trout was true. It sometimes had been hooked, so it was alleged, but had got away each time. Moreover it was said to have seized young ducks swimming on the loch waters.

Ascertaining from our host the situation of this loch we proceeded on our quest for it. Crossing over moorland we came to a cluster of crofters' houses, and situated right in the midst of them lay a small loch. It was evidently the one indicated by our friend; but it looked so small and insignificant that we much doubted the story of the fish we had heard. A man came out from a cottage door and Craig called out, 'Are there any fish in this loch?' The answer was 'Aye, but they are verra seldom.' We were soon carefully casting, and we methodically fished the whole of the water. The loch was so small that we thrice covered its surface in very short time, and though it was favourable weather for fishing, no sign of fish did we see. We left the loch with an impression of our having been 'taken in' by 'another fishing story'.

On several subsequent occasions, when my friend visited me, we fished this loch without obtaining any evidence of there being a fish in it. When on my way to other lochs lying south of the schoolhouse (*in Garrynamonie, south of Daliburgh*), I usually made a detour so as to make a few casts over the waters of this little loch, ever hopeful of getting a response as a reward for my perseverance. Fish life there always seemed to be non-existent, till one Saturday morning! As usual I had made my detour to the loch, rather as a matter of habit than with any expectation of a rise as I sent my flies out over the water. They fell lightly; there was a movement in the water and something had taken the middle fly off my cast! I struck, but the line met with a dead resistance and not a movement! At first I thought that the hook must be fixed into some inanimate object such as an old boot or a log. I tugged and pulled without response. Then the object (whatever it was beneath the surface I could not decide) began to move. There was no rush or plunge of a fish, but there was an irresistible force taking my steady gliding taut line through the water. I felt joy and pride for I did not doubt that I had hooked *the monster trout!* At the west end of the loch there were some bulrushes, and I began to fear the fish getting among them; so I gave him the butt of the rod and put on the utmost weight and pressure I dare. This made no impression whatever upon him! The fish's steady glide simply continued, up and down the loch, across it and back again; backwards and forwards it went at just the steady rate. For all the effect of my rod's pressure on him he might have been a sack of coal instead of a fish. I had met my master, and I now began to have the feeling that he was playing with me, and that he was amused at my efforts to disturb his imperturbability or to bring him to the water's surface – I was helpless against him! Suddenly as though weary with the game he had been playing, he stopped. Then he swam direct for the rushes at the end of the loch. Frantically I tugged, jerked and pulled with both hands; but I might as well have been trying to stop a horse! Without deviating in the least from his course, he headed directly into the bulrushed water. There my line became stationary. After my pulling very hard, it came away, was reeled in but minus the flies! My feelings may be better imagined than expressed as I ruefully gazed at the waters before me. During the whole of the time – (I was going to say 'that I was playing the fish' but, perhaps, 'that the fish was playing with me' would be more appropriate) – not a glimpse of the fish did I get, not even a fin; nor was there any swirl of water as the fish calmly turned in its course. I, and many others afterwards essayed to catch this 'demon trout'; but, as far as I learned, no one ever met with success.

Index of Lochs Mentioned

Index of Flies & Fly Patterns

The Collected Sayings of William Felton

On Other People's Ghillying

The engine won't work if you play Colonel Bogie with the choke.

Kenny, the boat's bolloxed.

On Fankles

Are you knitting or something?

I'll tell you how to straighten out that line. Grow runner beans up it. And buy a new one to fish with.

On His Military Experience

You can never fool an ex-Sergeant Major.

Give him a few years with me in the army.

I spent over 30 years building up a reputation as a hard man. If any of my squaddies saw me now, my reputation would be totally shot.

On Other People's Fishing

For a moment there I was quite impressed.

On His Own Fishing

If it wasn't for that bloody harrier, I'd have had that trout.

I've had three pounders in every part of this loch.

On Various Subjects

Bloody Rah-Rahs.

Watch out. There are some big fish in there.

Fifteen-Two, Fifteen-Four and One for his Nobs.

Tony, I told you to let them come within range.

Final Word

You never have a blank day on Bee.

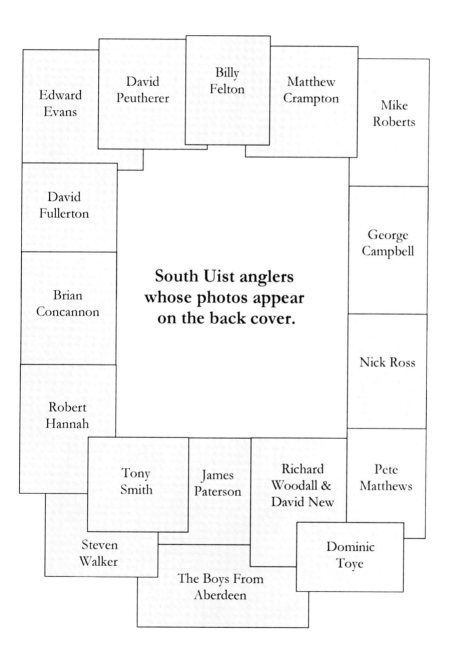

Edward Evans

David Peutherer

Billy Felton

Matthew Crampton

Mike Roberts

David Fullerton

George Campbell

Brian Concannon

South Uist anglers whose photos appear on the back cover.

Nick Ross

Robert Hannah

Tony Smith

James Paterson

Richard Woodall & David New

Pete Matthews

Steven Walker

Dominic Toye

The Boys From Aberdeen

159

Lightning Source UK Ltd.
Milton Keynes UK
UKOW031410071211

183362UK00011B/124/P